D0357298

EXPOSING THE MYTHS OF PARENTHOOD

In appreciation for your support of Focus on the Family, please accept this copy of *Exposing the Myths of Parenthood* by David Jeremiah. Your contributions enable this organization to address the needs of homes through radio, television, literature and counseling.

We are confident the information on the following pages will help you to become a more effective and fulfilled parent. With its practical advice, we believe this book will make a fine addition to your home library.

Focus on the Family
Pomona, CA 91799

EXPOSING THE
MYTHS
OF PARENTHOOD

DAVID JEREMIAH
with CAROLE C. CARLSON

WORD PUBLISHING
Dallas · London · Sydney · Singapore

Unless otherwise indicated, all Scripture quotations are taken from the Holy Bible,
New International Version, copyright © 1973, 1978, 1984 International Bible
Society. Used by permission of Zondervan Bible Publishers. Quotations identified
KJV are from The King James version of the Bible. Those identified TLB are from
The Living Bible, copyright 1971 by Tyndale House Publishers, Wheaton, IL.
Those identified NASB are from The New American Standard Bible, © The Lock-
man Foundation 1960, 1962, 1963, 1968, 1971, 1972, 1973, 1975, 1977.

Library of Congress Cataloging-in-Publication Data

Jeremiah, David.
    Exposing the Myths of Parenthood/David Jeremiah with Carole C. Carlson

        p.   cm.
    ISBN 0-8499-3087-1 (pbk.)
    1. Parenting.   2. Child rearing   I. Carlson, Carole C.   II. Title
    HQ755.8.J47   1988
    649.'.1—dc19   87-37154
                                                        CIP

8 9 8 0 1 2 3 9 AGF 9 8 7 6 5 4 3 2 1

Printed in the United States of America

To my children
JANICE, DAVID, JENNIFER, and DANIEL
the four best teachers
any two parents could hope for

Contents

INTRODUCTION xi

MYTH ONE: GOOD PARENTS DON'T HAVE
PROBLEMS WITH THEIR KIDS 1

• Lord, Lord, Have I Failed? • The Minute-by-Minute Manager
• A Page from the Journal of a Hurting Father • Facing Reality
• Train Up a Child • Effective or Delinquent Fathers • Business
First • All for Sex • Busy Doing God's Work • Do I Pass the
Test? • Guilt in the Trash Barrel • Who Is a Good Parent?
• Checklist for Parents Who Have Problems with Their Kids

MYTH TWO: TIME: IT'S NOT THE QUANTITY,
BUT THE QUALITY 23

• Myth Makers • But I'm Not a Sheepherder • Causes
of the Absentee-Parent Family • Building Special Times
• If Only . . .

MYTH THREE: SHE'S MOMMY'S GIRL 39

• What Are Fathers For? • Famous Fathers and Their
Daughters • Is Dad Really That Important? • Father/Daughter
Stages • Like Father/Like Daughter • Who Makes the Best
Dad? • But It's Never Too Late

MYTH FOUR: HE'S DADDY'S BOY 61

• Where Can You Find a Model Mother? • Blessed Among
Women • Where's Mom Today? • How Can Mothers Raise
Bold Leaders? • Biblical Principles of Success

MYTH FIVE: A CHAPTER A DAY KEEPS THE
DEVIL AWAY 77

• Stamping on Sacred Ground • God's Directions for Family
Devotions • Practical Lessons from Jewish Tradition • Practical
Lessons for Christians • A Night to Remember • Jesus, Our
Model • Four Reasons to Instill Christian Standards Today
• Another Myth: The Good Lord Rules in the Christian Schools

MYTH SIX: READ A BOOK AND RAISE A CHILD 99

• Keeping Our Balance in a Teeter-Totter World • To Love Is
to Discipline • The Good News Is Positive Discipline • It
Hurts • To Spank or Not • Do We Really Understand
Discipline? • The Power of Praise • Don't Give Up • Read
the Right Book and Raise a Child

MYTH SEVEN: TV DOESN'T AFFECT ME 119

• It's Not All Bad • Our Love-Hate Relationship • Mass
Hypnoses • Scratches on the TV Tray • The Subtle Battle
• Cold Turkey • Taming the Idol in the Box • Back to Balance

MYTH EIGHT: TEENS ARE TROUBLE 137

• Adolescence: A Twentieth Century Invention • Hurry
Up . . . Grow Up • Playing Fair in a Tug of War • Beneath
the Bravado • Give Me This Day • Out of the Frying Pan
• They're Wonderful . . . Tell Them • Addressed for Success

**MYTH NINE: WHEN THEY'RE GROWN THEY'RE
ON THEIR OWN** 157

• The Empty Nest Is an Illusion • Boomerang Kids • What the
Young Single Faces • Be It Ever So Humble • Leave and
Cleave • And Then There Were Three . . . Or More
• Identify Conflicts before They Become Problems • What
Our Kids Need When They're No Longer Kids

MYTH TEN: TO BE LOVED IS TO FEEL LOVED 173

• Jan's Story • The Next Chapter • How Do We Really Love Our
Kids? • He's Not Through with Me Yet • Parable of the Sad
Little Girl • A Special Kind of Love

NOTES 191

Introduction

Somewhere in the process of becoming a parent, I began to realize that it was not what I thought it would be. I was not disappointed as a father . . . not at all. I was just surprised. The reality I was learning to accept did not match my expectations.

From time to time, I would write down some of my discoveries. I shared these thoughts with friends and found out that many of my misconceptions about parenting had also crossed their minds.

But every time I tried to organize my ideas into an outline for a book, I was stopped short by my fears: *Who am I to be writing about the family? What if I get all of this published in a book and then experience difficulty with one of my children?*

For the last decade I have continued to record my own observations, collect appropriate articles, and *not* write a book! At first I pushed other writing projects ahead of this one and finally determined to leave the subject of the family to someone whose children had become adults and were serving God as missionaries in China or Africa. At least that father or mother might be able to attest to the results of the godly upbringing of their progeny.

Then the thing that I feared did happen. We encountered some serious problems in our family, and strange as it may seem, I realized at that time that I had to write this book.

During my family difficulties, I discovered that the suffering parent who goes to the bookstore looking for help often finds, instead, more reasons to feel guilty. Maybe it was time for someone to tell about the struggles as well as the triumphs of parenthood. When most people write about family life as they remember it, they write only of their successes. I can attest to the fact that parental pain is so severe that once it has subsided, it is repressed and forgotten.

In our own time of deepest hurt as parents, Donna and I learned there were families all around us who were experiencing many of the same challenges. If we had not been willing to swallow our pride and join a parent's support group, we would have struggled on as if we were the only hurting family on the planet. Instead, the mutual sharing in the group enabled us to put our own problems in perspective.

The summer before the release of this book, I was a speaker on the Bible conference circuit and talked about some of the concepts that we have included here. I was overwhelmed by the response. At the conclusion of my messages, couple after couple confided that they had never before been able to talk to anyone about the problems they were facing with their children.

I decided to write about the family as it really is for parents who are still involved in the process. Let's be honest, all of us struggled with our children at some time. While it is true that some of our heartaches are due to our own neglect or irresponsibility, the majority are the result of the faulty concepts that have shaped our image of parenthood. Our actions grow out of the assumptions we have made as we have grown into adulthood, and both are often passed on from one generation to the next without being questioned! More than we know, we are controlled by our misbeliefs.

In the pages that follow, I have written about some of my misbeliefs. I have called them myths, for a myth is a belief, thought to be accurate, but existing only in one's memory or imagination. Especially in the early years of my family responsibility, I allowed these myths to adversely affect my home.

As you read this book, I pray that you will realize you are not alone in your journey through the challenging years of family life. As parents we have much in common! We can learn from our own mistakes, and if we are willing to risk our reputations as parents, we can help others learn from our mistakes as well.

In the months before we committed to write this book, God brought Ward and Carole Carlson into our lives. Whenever the Jeremiahs got together with the Carlsons, we felt a unique bond. Ward and Carole scheduled a week at the Forest Home Summer Bible Conference when I was one of the speakers, and it was then that I told Carole about my ideas for this book and asked her if she would work with me on the project. I was concerned that I might not be able to write objectively about my own family. When Carole said she would help, we met with Ernie Owen and Dick Baltzell of Word, and they gave us the green light.

My wife's name does not appear on the front cover of this book, but you will quickly discover that Donna is an author in her own right. She is the only person with whom I have shared the tears and laughter that are revealed in these chapters. For twenty-five years she has been my wife, my best friend, and the co-producer of the Jeremiah children.

Dr. Ken Nichols, a Christian psychologist and close personal friend, read the manuscript, and his helpful suggestions have become a part of the finished product. Tom Thompson, one of my associates in the pastoral ministry, has taught family seminars in hundreds of churches across America. His enthusiasm for this project has been a great encouragement. And I also extend my sincere thanks and appreciation to Glenda Parker, my administrative assistant who coordinated all of the creative sessions, made helpful suggestions, and stayed on top of the myriad details that might have been overlooked.

Most of all, I want to express my deep love to our four children. There is a wonderful joy in our home. It has always been there, but it has increased as we have come to understand that we all—parents and children—are growing up together.

MYTH ONE

Good Parents
Don't Have Problems
With Their Kids

*T*he story begins uneventfully, a smooth sea with no clouds on the horizon. When I left the church office that morning everything was calm—no major crises, nothing to forewarn me of the events to come. I had been visiting one of our members in the hospital and was driving back to work with images of pain and suffering lingering in my mind. I almost felt ashamed of my own good health. Although I could sympathize with the discomfort and even the agony of those who were struggling with their anxieties or fears, I found it difficult to empathize. I had never experienced severe or life-threatening illness.

It's not my nature to dwell upon depressive thoughts, so I began to plan my study time on the life of Joseph. I relished the thought of beginning to preach these new messages with their time-proven truths. Looking at my watch, I thought I would have three uninterrupted hours to work before an afternoon meeting. The road wasn't crowded, so I was enjoying the drive in my big blue van, designed to transport and entertain our family of six—plus various friends and pets. We had a lot of fun on trips in this little bus. I cruised along quietly, allowing the warm California sun to infuse me with well-being. It was a temporary reprieve before the storm.

My car phone (an important new luxury for this preacher on the move over the endless freeways) rang, jarring me out of my daydreaming. My secretary's voice came through with unmistakable urgency.

"Pastor, you need to get back to your office as soon as you can. Randy is here and Jan is in trouble."

My recent hospital visit flashed through my mind; had my lovely daughter been in an accident? My hands tightened on the wheel. "What kind of trouble?"

Glenda was a calm woman, used to handling all types of church

3

emergencies, but this time her voice was breaking. "Jan hasn't been hurt," she said, almost reading my thoughts, "but Randy needs to talk with you. He said he would wait."

I probably drove faster than I should, thinking of all the kinds of trouble a young person could get into that would cause Randy, the Superintendent of Schools, to call. Was it cheating? Morality? I pushed all my grim thoughts away. It must be some minor infraction of the rules, some teenage caper that could mean a temporary grounding. It couldn't be too serious, I told myself.

When I reached the office, Randy was waiting. One look at the sober expression on his face, and I knew this would not be a minor problem.

"I just don't know how to tell you this," he said, "but we've just learned that several of our high school students decided to experiment with cocaine. Jan was one of those who admitted trying the drug, and we had to expel her, along with the others."

I must have stared at him in disbelief. But I knew he would not have brought me this jolting news without solid verification. *Oh, Jan, why did you do such a foolish thing? Was this the first time or had there been others?* The consequences flashed through my mind like a screeching siren in the night. How would my wife, Donna, cope with this? What about our other children? What publicity would be brought on Christian High, and especially the preacher's kid? Sure, I even thought about what it would mean for the preacher.

The feelings that overwhelmed me when I heard Randy's words were unlike anything in my previous experience—even the times on the basketball court when I had been knocked to the floor, gasping for breath and wondering if I could ever get up, or the night Donna and I had wept together over the death of our unborn baby. Over the years I had counseled with many distraught and hurting parents and children, but nothing in my life had prepared me for the initial shock and the resulting pain of the days and months to follow.

LORD, LORD, HAVE I FAILED?

When Jan was expelled from school, everyone knew. A large newspaper carried the story, and although names were not used because the girls involved were minors, the article mentioned that the daughter of a pastor was involved. It didn't take a sleuth to know who that could be. A brush fire during the California dry season could not have spread faster.

On the Sunday after the announcement of the expelling, I preached on "The Advantage of Adversity." I choked back tears throughout the message. People in the congregation knew what was happening, and I sensed their care and concern. I confess that I had an overwhelming sense of failure as a father; I even considered resigning from the church (many pastors I have known who have had trouble with their children *have* resigned). I knew of a pastor who handed in his resignation to his elders, but they wouldn't accept it. Maybe, I thought, that would happen to me.

There is a biblical passage that gives guidelines for a church leader (whether he is a deacon, an elder, a pastor, or a teacher) in a situation like mine. It is found in 1 Timothy 3:4–5. I reexamined that command: "He must manage his own family well and see that his children obey him with proper respect. (If anyone does not know how to manage his own family, how can he take care of God's church?)"

Does that mean all of my children have to be paragons of virtue? Does this command put a P.K. (preacher's kid, for those who haven't been brought up as one) under unreasonable pressure? Unfortunately, tradition in many churches has made this so. I believe that managing my family well means not neglecting my duties as a father, but working through the problems when they arise. In fact, if I understand management at all, it exists to deal with problems. A manager who has no problems to solve is soon out of work. We never prove our managerial skills better than when we are giving direction or perspective in the midst of turmoil.

We wanted to help Jan, and at the same time have her and our other children, David, Daniel, and Jennifer, understand that our love for them is not based on a performance scale or perfect behavior. If it were, none of us would be acceptable in God's kingdom.

THE MINUTE-BY-MINUTE MANAGER

At first I couldn't talk to anyone except Donna about the anguish in my heart. After a time, we were able to meet with Dr. Ken

Nichols, a trusted Christian counselor, who over the days and weeks to follow helped Jan, Donna, and me work through some decisions we had to make. I had counseled many families myself, but now I was sitting on the other side of the desk. Too often I've seen parents keep their problems bottled up, either out of embarrassment or the belief that they could handle their difficulties alone. I understood my emotions of shame and pride, but I knew we needed some professional counsel to help us think through our options.

Just as we were beginning to see progress, another crisis would arise. Experimenting with cocaine was not an incident as much as it was a symptom. My Jan was really struggling with her life, and something had to be done. I remember telling her that all the Band-Aids in my box were gone . . . temporary measures were not bringing the needed results, and Jan was just as miserable with the treatment as we were.

Finally, I made one of the most difficult decisions of my life. After Jan had been readmitted to school on probation, she violated yet another rule, and that's when we sat down with her one day and said, "Jan, you blew it, and we have to deal with it." I believed in what the school stood for, and as both a board member and her father I had to make some hard decisions. We took her out of school. It was a gloomy day for this dad, in spite of the California sunshine.

I asked our counselor, "Do you think she could stay at home, and you could counsel with her, and she could get over this?"

"David," he replied, "As much as I want to be an encouragement, it seems to me something more than a routine counseling approach will be needed. We can't control her environment. All we could do is talk and hope."

Within a few weeks' time we confronted three major family problems, unrelated to the challenges with Jan. Each time the strain on our family was compounded. We realized that Jan needed to go someplace where she could live and study and grow in a different environment, away from peer pressure, church scrutiny, and her high-profile family. So we decided to send her to school in the Dominican Republic. But that is part of Jan's story which she will tell later. I can only try to describe how I felt.

For seven days in a row I woke up crying. Donna and I know there is no pain like parental pain; it tears at your insides when you love your children so intensely. However, I poured my heart out to the Lord, and He revealed a truth to me I had never understood before.

A PAGE FROM THE JOURNAL OF A HURTING FATHER

"These last few days, Lord, have been so difficult. Little did I know when I began to speak on 'Stress' that I would experience the things which have happened. This whole situation with Jan has totally devastated me. I have been unable to pray for these last three days. Lord, I don't understand if I have been ashamed to come to You because I feel so responsible, or if it's just that the hurt is so great. I have been neutralized.

"Lord, I love my Jan so much . . . I believed in her and she was not honest with me. How can I recover what has been lost? Lord, help me know what to do. Lord, make me willing to be vulnerable and see what I have done to contribute to this situation . . . God, help Donna and Jan to make it through these difficult days together. Don't let anything come between us that would further complicate things for our family.

"Lord Jesus, I realize that these notes are about our relationship, Yours and mine . . . I cannot lose sight of the fact that the lesson for me behind all of this is the fact that what I feel now as a hurting father is how You must feel when I have been unfaithful to You. . . . I guess I have never really sensed that before. But now I feel at the deepest level of my life the hurt and loss that must fill Your heart for me so many times.

"Oh God, forgive me for bringing such pain to Your life as I have felt . . . help me never to forget what this feels like. Lord, please help me to help Jan. May this be the beginning of new things for her life and mine."

FACING REALITY

When I began in the ministry, I had four theories on child-raising and no children; now I have four children and no theories.

One of my notions was that if I did my very best to be a good parent, watched my role models, and followed biblical principles,

Donna and I would have no problems with our children. Some of them might even follow me in the ministry, just as I had followed my father. What else would you expect with a name like ours?

As our children and our churches grew, I began to see the breakdown of the myths surrounding the Christian family. Many of these fables had caused parents both guilt and confusion because their offspring didn't follow the expected patterns of behavior; the theories we heard and believed didn't seem to match our experience.

I'm not a psychologist or an expert on child behavior. I'm a Christian pastor, the husband of one beautiful wife, and the father of two daughters and two sons. What I have learned is that I need to be learning. Ben Franklin once told about a boy who was so smart he could name a horse in nine languages, but so ignorant he bought a cow to ride on. I may be riding on the backs of a few sacred cows in this book.

Trying to demythologize some of the myths of parenthood might establish my foolishness, but I'm prepared to be the target, if the arrows aren't too sharp.

TRAIN UP A CHILD

Life is a classroom, and the courses will be tough at times; however, sometimes we find what we have been taught doesn't seem to provide the answers in the test of life. Parents may be like computers that come out with garbled results because the input was interpreted improperly. We have been told to "Train up a child in the way he should go: and when he is old, he will not depart from it" (Proverbs 22:6, KJV). In my background, Proverbs have been repeated and quoted for many of life's situations, and if it is a Proverb, it must be right. Wrong. Before I am branded a heretic, look with me more carefully at this important verse.

I believe what Proverbs 22:6 says about child-raising has been communicated inadequately to parents. The time-worn and often-taught interpretation of this verse is: even though my child may be wayward now, he will come back to the Lord in his later life, and we will be vindicated as parents. I must admit I have never found a great deal of comfort in this message. Even if the normal application were accurate, for many parents of prodigals, vindication would come too late for it to be enjoyed in this life.

Is Proverbs 22:6 a hard and fast formula for successful parenting? I don't think so! To follow such logic would be to unravel the meaning of the entire book. Proverbs is an inspired collection of observations, most of which were made by the wisest man who ever lived. The book is the Word of God, but it must be properly interpreted to be understood! As a personal test, try your inflexible logic on these:

— Does everyone who keeps God's Law receive long life (Proverbs 3:2)?

— Does every wise son make his father glad (Proverbs 10:1)?

— Does every godly man live long and every wicked man die young (Proverbs 10:27)?

— Do all lazy people fail (Proverbs 12:24)?

There are more proverbs to prove the same point. Christian psychiatrist John White agrees:

What about Proverbs 22:6? If you examine its context, you will discover that the verse is not a promise made by God to anybody. It is a statement, a general statement about how family relationships normally work . . . it tells us what we can see around us if we only open our eyes. Good parents usually produce good children . . . but when we interpret it as inflexible law, we are reading into it something the Holy Spirit never intended.[1]

Even if this were an unconditional promise, we have missed the way! This Proverb has some very clear prerequisites before we can claim it in relationship to our children. For instance, we all make these kinds of promises: "Eat everything on your plate and then you can have dessert." "Finish your homework and pick up your room and then you can go out." The idea of training up a child (or teenager) has some provisions attached to it.

Many times accurate biblical meaning does not translate easily into modern language. When you hear your pastor refer to words in the original Hebrew or Greek, don't tune him out. He's not trying to show off his seminary knowledge; he is attempting to communicate the exact meaning of a passage. To the twentieth century listener, "train up" sounds like a corrective disciplinary action. Of course we correct or discipline, but we also prevent. Discipline is an integral part of Proverbs: "Folly is bound up in the heart of a child, but the rod of discipline will drive it far from him" (Proverbs 22:15). Unfortunately, far too much discipline today, even by Christian parents, falls into the category of the corrective, and not the preventive. We have been quick to build hospitals at the bottom of the cliff, but we fail to see the necessity of building fences at the top.

The Hebrew word for "train up" is used only four other times in the Scriptures. It is used twice in Deuteronomy 20:5 of a man dedicating his new home. Later it is used in 1 Kings 8:63 and 2 Chronicles 7:5 of King Solomon dedicating the house of God. Here's the clue on training: parents are told to dedicate their children to the Lord and show complete dependence upon Him. That's the tough part. We may say that we dedicate our kids to the Lord, but then we kidnap them away from Him as soon as the going gets rough. "If the Bible says we are to train and discipline our children, then they should do what we say, no questions asked!" This is the attitude that has developed in many evangelical families as a result of a reaction against our permissive society. "Train up" is sometimes replaced with a sharp, "Shape up!"

> We may say that we dedicate our kids to the Lord, but then we kidnap them away from Him as soon as the going gets rough.

Contrary to what we may believe *training* means, the term used in the Bible has as its root meaning the words for "palate or roof of the mouth." In Job 34:3 and Psalms 119:103, we find references to taste or "honey to the mouth." The picture is this: the Arab midwife would take olive oil or crushed dates on her finger and rub the palate of a newborn baby to create in the infant a desire to suck. The real meaning of *training* is to create a taste or desire.

Our responsibility as parents is to develop in our children a hunger, taste, or desire for spiritual things. This is not the picture of "you do as I say," but a process of cultivating the personal urge to love God and follow Him. Honey on the palate will develop a taste for sweetness.

Do we train or force feed? Sometimes, I must admit, it's a little of both. I can remember the old baby-food days, when we would tease our little highchair persons with a spoonful of applesauce—and shove the spinach or beets in before they knew what was happening. However, as babies grow older, forced feeding doesn't work. There have been times when Donna and I have been criticized because we have not made our children attend a certain church service or sit through a long sermon (even when Dad is preaching). On the other hand, there are some church functions our kids never want to miss.

That brings me to another way in which many of us have misinterpreted the most-quoted child-raising proverb: "Train up a child in the way he should go. . . ." The Hebrew word or phrase for "in the way" describes the habit or character of an individual at his own age level. The emphasis is on the importance of adjusting our training according to the ability of a child at each stage in his development. Children do not come in standard packages; each child is different, and we parents need to study the "labels." Bringing up a child in the way he should go is not an unchangeable mathematical equation. Comparing one child with another is like buying two products in the market: they may be processed by the same manufacturer, have similar boxes, but taste entirely different. Each child has his own way, and by listening, or even keeping a diary of behavior patterns, we can begin to determine what that way is.

Kids function on different wavelengths: one may be so sensitive that just a word or even a look tells him he's doing something wrong. Another will be defensive and make excuses: it wasn't his fault, or circumstances forced him into a situation. For instance, there's this bit of illogic: "What was I to do? Everyone was in the car and wanted to go to the drive-in. How was I to know it was an 'R' rated movie? I was stuck." Other kids seem immune to punishment. I can remember spanking my daughter Jennifer when she was little and she never cried; her face was so stoic I couldn't help admiring her composure. Then when I stopped, put my arms around her and told her I loved her, "Niagara Falls" spilled over.

Parenting is not an easy formula; the Bible gives us the major principles, but the application is different for everyone.

"Train up a child in the way he should go, and when he is old. . . ." gives us the conditional promise which is linked to the beginning of the proverb. If when our children are small, and on through their youth, we give them a real taste or desire for the things of the Lord, then when they become old, they will not want to turn aside from these things.

"That's not true!" you may say. "I know kids who have been brought up in good Christian homes who have gone completely sour in every aspect of their lives." You're right. This promise does not *guarantee* that a lost or backslidden son or daughter will be saved or return to a desire for spiritual values. The principle of sowing and reaping is valid in all our lives—even the lives of our children.

God gave us all a free will, and we can't use it if we have not been given choices; however, a course in "Comparative Religion" does not offer honest alternatives. The truth of the gospel of Jesus Christ and a personal relationship with Him cannot be compared to a mere involvement in some religious practice. Children need to learn about Jesus, attend a church where the Bible is taught, and know how to accept Him through a confession of faith.

If our parental guideline proverb is paraphrased to give it the impact of its meaning, it might say: "If you dedicate your child to the Lord and create within him a desire for spiritual things in accord with his age level, you have given him the best possible opportunity to grow into spiritual maturity." Solomon wasn't as wordy, but I believe that is a fair interpretation of what he meant.

EFFECTIVE OR DELINQUENT FATHERS

If you've never had a broken leg, it's difficult to understand the discomfort, the itching cast, the awkward movements. For years I had counseled parents in pain, many of them with problems more complex than ours. Although I felt burdened for them and their families, I had not walked in their shoes until now. Many times a counselor is able to see a pattern of parental indifference or neglect, of permissiveness or harshness, but other times the examination reveals that parents were doing their best and didn't know where they had gone wrong.

Dr. Charlie Shedd tells of an experience he had on a plane, jetting to Los Angeles. He was seated next to a well-dressed man who was absorbed in an article, graphically illustrated with pictures of teenagers on drugs. When he finished reading, the young man closed the magazine and stared into space. Apparently forgetting those around him, he half-spoke, half-whispered what seemed to be a prayer. "Oh God—I wonder why! I suppose nobody knows." And then he added quickly, "But if a father can make the difference, I sure want to make the difference!"

Dr. Shedd could not ignore the man's concern, so he began to ask him questions. He learned that he was a successful businessman, who was burdened by the demands of his career. He had a wife and three children, and nothing was higher on his agenda for the years ahead than to be an effective father—a father who would "make the difference."

Many fathers fail because they underestimate their task. If they pay their bills and make everyday decisions, they think the long-range plan will come out all right. But often it does not work that way; the rate of failure among fathers is at an all-time high. Just look at the number of women who are raising their families alone, playing the demanding dual roles of both father and mother.

The standard for an effective dad is higher than that of most corporate presidents. A job description for a father might read: "The father must be a man of vision, strength, and character, capable of leading an in-service training organization that will in time reproduce parents like himself. He must carry on his training at all age levels. He must be able to cooperate effectively with his help-mate, give advice and counsel as needed, and provide spiritual help and leadership. He must care for his own personal problems, prepare his own budgets, and maintain good public relations. He must be a qualified service and repair man. He must be willing to do whatever is needed 24 hours a day, 365 days a year. Finally, he must provide his own salary as well as the financial needs of the entire organization."

As I thought more about being a father, I looked in the Scriptures to find some good role models, men who had the right approach to this career. I seemed to find more evidence of men who fell short of God's standard of parenting than those who met it. Their mistakes and shortcomings were the same as those of twentieth century dads.

BUSINESS FIRST

By today's standards, we would consider Lot a great real estate salesman or business executive. His story, recorded in chapter 13 of the book of Genesis, contains more than his wife being turned into a pillar of salt.

Lot came out of Egypt with his Uncle Abraham, loaded with all the wealth the world could afford. He had so many possessions that he had to come to terms with Abraham and separate from him. From that time onward, Lot went downhill; his relationship with both his uncle and his God began to crumble. At first he "pitched his tent toward Sodom," one of the most wicked towns of his time. (Even to this day, the very name, "Sodom," epitomizes the worst in man.) It wasn't long before he moved into the city and became one of its leading citizens.

When God decided to destroy Sodom and Gomorrah, He sent messengers to Lot to warn him that the cities were going to be judged with fire. Lot knew the messengers were telling the truth, so he hurried to his daughters, who had married men from Sodom, and warned them of the impending doom. Some of the saddest words in the Bible are found in Genesis 19:14: "He [Lot] said, 'Hurry and get out of this place, because the Lord is about to destroy the city!' But his sons-in-law thought he was joking." His own family did not believe his warning! In his desire to get wealth, property, and prestige in the city, Lot had lost his credibility with those closest to him. He had traded influence with his children for prestige in the world.

In the last episode recorded in the life of this man, we read that he committed incest with his daughters. Somewhere between the journey out of Egypt and his occupancy of a place at the city gate in Sodom, Lot "lost" his family. Power and money were more important than his role as an effective father.

ALL FOR SEX

David was a king—a great leader of men; he was brilliantly gifted with power, wealth, and creative talent. However, because of lust and desire for another man's wife, David committed adultery and as a result gave up godly influence in his own home. His family's story is tragic because it is filled with disaster. Here was a king of Israel, representing God to His people, and yet we read of terrible things happening to his progeny. Amnon, David's son, fell in love with his sister Tamar, and when she would not respond to him, Amnon raped her. Consequently, Absalom, David's other son, was so infuriated that he had Amnon killed by Joab, David's general. Later, Absalom was also killed by Joab.

Today we see men in government leadership ruining their careers with sexual encounters. The greater tragedy is to see what is happening when trusted Christian leaders fall into adultery, destroying their ministries and their families in the process.

My lifestyle has nothing in common with Lot or David, but at times I wonder if there are other ways I have fallen short of God's requirements for a father.

BUSY DOING GOD'S WORK

Every person who finds himself overcommitted in church work or other types of Christian service should study the life of Eli, the priest. This father was one of God's men, a priest in Israel, who served and sacrificed before the Lord God. However, he failed to meet God's standard for effective parenting. "Eli's sons were wicked men; they had no regard for the Lord" (1 Samuel 2:12). The word was out in Shiloh that Eli's boys were not just worthless, they were evil. What a terrible reputation for anyone's children, but it is even worse when they are the offspring of a man of God!

What those young men were doing must have been common knowledge because Scripture tells us they committed adultery with women at the door of the temple where their father ministered. And they extorted money from the townspeople. The astounding fact is that Eli didn't seem to know what his sons were doing. When he was old, he confronted them and said, "I hear from all the people about these wicked deeds of yours. No, my sons; it is not a good report that I hear spreading among the Lord's people" (1 Samuel 2:23–24). Where were you, Eli, that someone needed to tell you what was going on in your own family?

The key verse in the life of Eli tells us: "His sons, however, did not listen to their father's rebuke" (1 Samuel 2:25). Here was a man who had gained influence in spiritual leadership, but had traded it for the influence he should have had with his sons. He was capable of administering the priesthood and caring for the temple sacrifice, he was respected by all of the people, but in the process of spiritual leadership he had given up all that was important—his own sons.

Because Eli hadn't done his work at home, God cut off the priesthood from his line and gave it to another.

What went wrong in Eli's home? The similarities to what is happening to many homes in America are convincing. First, the priest of Israel vacated the priesthood of his own home. He was so busy taking care of the temple that he neglected his house. It sounds like the whimper of the modern father who says, "I'm not a churchgoing man; I leave religion to the wife and kids." Today the fatherly priesthood in our homes is a lost art.

However, there is at least one notable exception to the family pattern in modern America, and that is the Orthodox Jew. His example is particularly instructive, for these families frequently make their homes in urban ghettos—a place where many people find it difficult, if not impossible, to maintain a decent family life. Yet, because of their faithful dedication to Jewish family traditions, these fathers are influential leaders in their homes. The tragedy in these Jewish homes is of a different nature; they wait for a Messiah who has already come. However, there is a Christian tragedy, too: having accepted the heart of Judaism for our own, we have failed to maintain many of the ancient, strengthening traditions of Jewish family life.

Another fault of Eli is that he did not restrain the sin in his own home. The man of influence in the temple had lost his authority with his children.

DO I PASS THE TEST?

When things go wrong we are prone to self-examination. I need to examine my parenting score frequently. Am I "too busy" or over-committed or self-centered? Am I giving more of myself to people outside my family than I am to Donna and the kids? If I evaluate my performance candidly, line it up against some star players, how do I rate? There were times when I was sure I was a good parent, and other times when I began to wonder.

As both Donna and I look back on our days with Jan, we do not have any difficulty finding our mistakes. Jan was our first child and sometimes we were not sure of what we were doing. We made mistakes, lots of them. I did not take the time I should have in the beginning. (When Jan was little, I was in the process of starting a church in Indiana, and the schedule I imposed upon myself left little time for home and family. I corrected that later, but Jan was older by then.) I did not always understand what was going on in Jan's life, but I did not always try to find out, either. Sometimes, I would just throw up my hands in frustration. "Girls . . . who can understand them at all?"

I am sure I identified more with my boys at the beginning. I thought this was normal and right. I learned later how wrong I was. We did not pray enough with or for Jan. (That statement is guaranteed to make every parent wince with guilt and anguish.) Sometimes I lost my cool and raised my voice . . . and I am sure I could list many other shortcomings as well.

Yes, we make mistakes and we know it. But are we responsible? Does all the blame rest on us? Not one of us really believes that anymore.

Donna and I were advised to become involved with the parents of other children who were experiencing struggles and had enrolled their children in the same school as Jan's. When we attended our first group meeting I was very embarrassed; it was a very awkward situation for us. I wondered if they knew I was a pastor or had seen our television program. My pride was showing its ugly side, but we soon got over that when we discovered no one really cared who we were, what prestige we had or didn't have, or whether we had money or not. All of us parents had some things in common; we loved our children and wanted to help them. After hearing some stories from other parents, I didn't think ours was nearly as bad.

As our support group became more open, we discovered the great therapeutic value of sharing with others. Honesty and transparency, however, must be combined with confidentiality and a nonjudgmental attitude. One of the greatest discoveries we made is that our problems were not unique.

One of the challenges of being a pastor is this: you may well be the only member of the church who doesn't have a pastor. It was during this period in my life that a minister in our city reached out to me and provided the friendship and encouragement I needed. George Gregg is the pastor of Faith Chapel in San Diego; he phoned me regularly, prayed for me, and reminded me that it wasn't the end of the world. When he knew he was going to be out of town for two weeks, he called to say he would be praying and would get in touch when he returned. What a blessing it is to have someone stand by and support you when you're having a rough time.

GUILT IN THE TRASH BARREL

If we believe we have done our best as parents and things still go wrong, then we should release the guilt and get on with the recovery. I will never forget that first Christmas Jan was away from home after our decision that she needed to have a new, structured environment in which to grow. It was Christmas Eve, and my message was entitled "Being Away from Home." I began by reading the lines of the song "I'll Be Home for Christmas." Poor Donna, I don't know how she sat through that evening. However, I guess for the first time I really thought about what it would be like to be away from home for Christmas.

> If we believe we have done our best as parents and things still go wrong, then we should release the guilt and get on with the recovery.

The whole Christmas story is about being away from home; Joseph and Mary were away from their home, the angels were away from their heavenly home, and the wise men came from other lands. Jesus Himself was away from home. In all my ministry I had repeated the fact that God gives us trials to teach us, but many times we refuse to voice the lessons we have learned. That Christmas Eve I became vulnerable and discovered that people accept this in a pastor. Our church family prayed for us and for Jan. Many of them wrote to her. The criticism I had feared in my heart never materialized, for who is going to be critical? Will someone who has had children be critical? Will someone who is in the process of raising children be critical? We are all problems in process of being shaped by the Master.

Evelyn Christenson wrote: "We need to replace our impatience over the teen's behavior with an absolute assurance that the child is going to come back. This may mean paying a costly price in disciplined prayer and letting the Lord change us. It's much easier to be disgruntled parents and just throw up our hands in defeat. . . . No matter what the child does, we can still love him. We don't have to condone his behavior, but we can continue to love him."[2]

WHO IS A GOOD PARENT?

Good parents admit they're far from perfect. They're just trying to do their best. They read the books, try to follow biblical guidelines, and listen to their consciences. But many times the formula doesn't produce the expected results. Somewhere in the laboratory of living an ingredient is added which changes the chemistry. We look at all the components, examine each one, and say, "What went wrong?" The cake fell; the paint ran; the stage lights went out before the play ended.

But that's okay. Good parents can have problems with their kids. (And good kids can have problems with their parents!) With the permission of the other five members of my family, I want to help dispel some myths which have established a performance expectancy level most of us are unable to meet. The rigidity of the rules system on parenthood has brought many of us to the breaking point. However, one of the great things about God is that He can make something beautiful out of chaos. We'll experience both soaring and crashing, pride and disappointment; we can count on it.

Dr. James Dobson says, "There's hardly a parent alive who does not have some regrets and painful memories of failures as a mother or a father. Children are infinitely complex, and we cannot be perfect parents any more than we can be perfect human beings. We don't always handle our children as unemotionally as we wish we had, and it's very common to look back a year or two later and see how wrong we were in the way we approached a problem.

"All of us experience these failures! No one does the job perfectly!"[3]

If you just look around, you will discover that Dr. Dobson is right. Joe and Mary Lou Bayly raised five children to young adulthood; Joe was used mightily by God as a writer and leader. Just before his death, he wrote these words: "It is Mary Lou's and my opinion that in today's climate most parents—including Christian ones—who have more than one child will have at least one who causes 'ripples' while going through the teen age. For some, those ripples will continue into young adulthood."[4]

As I have traveled, I have met some of the most godly people who have suffered through the pain of parental disappointment. If I named these people, you would recognize them; they are leaders, writers, pastors, missionaries, and key laymen. They have suffered greatly, and sometimes I think it doesn't make sense.

On the other hand, I have known some of the most godly kids who have come out of the homes of profligate parents. Looking at their homes, I cannot explain it! They seem to have used their family misery as a goad to godliness and maturity. It is just not true that good parents always raise trouble-free children. The theory won't stand up. And we're just as wrong to accept all the blame for our children when they fail, as we are to accept all the credit for them when they succeed.

Sociologist Anthony Campolo writes: "It should be noted that God had two perfect children, Adam and Eve, whom he reared in the perfect environment of Eden; yet both of them rebelled against His will. Where there is freedom, there will be rebellion."[5]

What do we do, parents? Are there any practical guidelines to follow during the trying, crying times? Here are some suggestions that may be useful when and if you are searching for help:

CHECKLIST FOR PARENTS WHO HAVE PROBLEMS WITH THEIR KIDS

1. Our number-one priority is to *restore the relationship* with the child. Sometimes when a child gets into trouble, the parent wants to kick him out or have nothing to do with him. When a family goes through a period of rebellion with a child, it is important to say, "There's not anything you can do to make us stop loving you."

2. *Reinforce the spouse or parent.* When we knew Jan needed to go away to school, Donna and I had to support and reinforce each other. My experience as a pastor has been that quite often when there is a problem with a child, it ends up as a divisive element in the relationship between a husband and wife. Everyone needs reinforcement and affirmation; if a parent is alone, he or she needs a

friend, another member of the family, or a trusted counselor who can provide this kind of support.

3. We need to *refocus on the rest of the family.* When a problem surfaces, we end up spending an inordinate amount of time with that one member. As we were working through the details on how we were going to help Jan, we needed to stop and regroup as a family with David, Jennifer, and Daniel.

4. *Reevaluate our responsibility* in the situation. Did I make mistakes? What was my part in all this? We need to reassess and review our own performance.

5. *Refuse false hope.* There are no easy solutions. Some misguided counselors will give a set formula or a list of simple things to make a problem go away; but we must avoid hanging on to such false hope. Change will not come without new direction.

6. *Reach out for help.* I found it hard to do this. In a recent study it was disclosed that upper- to middle-class families have a greater sense of guilt about their problems with their children because of all of the advantages they have had; lower-class families accept problems with their offspring as a part of life and move on. When we need help, we should seek the best we can find.

7. *Reject false guilt.* We may agonize and accuse ourselves of those things over which we either had no control or those which we realize were mistakes. Guilt is one of the most debilitating of all emotions.

8. *Review our alternatives.* In every situation, the alternatives to inaction must be weighed against the possibilities of healing and restoration through action.

No matter what the problems may be, we cannot allow them to control our lives. I know that is something easier said than done, for this preacher has to remind himself to practice what he preaches and to see the advantages in adversity.

MYTH TWO

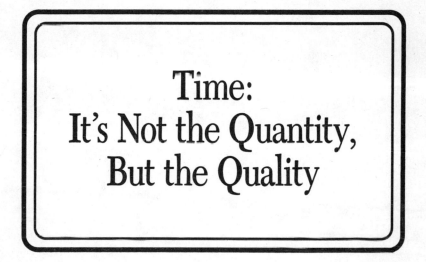

Time:
It's Not the Quantity,
But the Quality

*P*eople leave the Midwest to escape winter; they move to California, unpack mittens and woollies, and then bundle up again to search for the nearest snow. We hate the cold when we live in it and miss it when we leave it. The Jeremiah family had moved from Indiana to the mild climate of San Diego when a friend suggested we use his camp in the mountains for a time of family fun. We read those bumper stickers which said "Think Snow" and followed the suggestion. We hoped our good thoughts would turn into reality. The kids were excited about the adventures of exploring new territory; Donna and I needed a change after the demands of moving and getting into my new job. Our expectations were high.

The camp was beautiful, nestled in a little valley down a deeply rutted road. Cowboy actor Tim Holt had once owned the place, and his little white cottage was a miniature museum of western folklore. The children enjoyed several hours of horseback riding before we had to head back home (they knew that Saturday night was early-to-bed for this preacher's family). It was a fun time and we enjoyed being together. We laughed when Danny was given some slobbery lickings by a shaggy, overfriendly dog. And we doubled over at the shocked expression on Jennifer's face when her gentle Shetland pony broke into a trot. Poor David, no matter how loud he shouted, could not make his stubborn horse budge; he might as well have been sitting astride a wooden animal on a stalled carousel. It was a time that made me feel as good as hot coffee on a cold day.

As we pulled onto the main highway that would take us back home, I thought how hard it had been to have these family outings during the first few weeks of our ministry in a new church. How grateful I was at that moment for my loving wife, a beautiful family, and the day we had enjoyed together.

As we drove up the mountain that morning, I had promised that on the way home we would take a closer look at the snow along the highway. When I pulled over, everyone, except Donna, jumped out of the car to wade through the rapidly melting slush and pack a few snowballs. I warned the children to stay away from the road, since cars and trucks were zooming down the incline from the 4,000-foot summit.

Intent on repaying my older son for his icy direct hit on my forehead, I turned my back just as Jennifer, who barely came up to my waist, began to run toward the highway. Donna, who was sitting in the car, saw the impending danger and honked the horn; I spun around, shouting as I ran toward our little girl and pulled her to the other side of the car. I was shaking half in fear and half in anger when I applied my hand to her bottom and scolded her for disobeying. I buckled her firmly into her seat belt, and we endured the next few miles in complete silence, except for an occasional whimper from one small child huddled behind me.

After we had driven for a while, I stopped the car and had Jennifer climb over and sit next to me. She reluctantly obeyed. As I always try to do after punishment has been administered, I whispered in her ear how much I loved her and told her how frightened she made me by her careless act. I hugged her to me with one arm, while steering with the other, and, for some reason, began to choke back emotion.

I'm not absolutely certain what was happening to me at that moment; so many thoughts seemed to converge, creating a strange montage of my family in my mind—the day we had enjoyed together, the laughter, the fear, the sense of guilt because there had not been more days like this one. I was gripped with the painful thought of losing one of our children.

That drive home has been replayed in my mind many times; I'm not sure why the events of one day affected me as they did. I believe, however, that the essence of this whole chapter was condensed into those brief moments of reflection. What would happen in my family if the intensity of feeling and concern over the possible loss of my daughter were translated into the daily commitment involved in being a father? Why does it take a traumatic experience to show us how important our children are? When will we learn that their loss would be no less painful if it were because of neglect rather than tragedy?

.MYTH MAKERS

"It's not the quantity but the quality of time that really counts." I believe the first time I heard that statement was in a seminary classroom. I'm not sure I really believed it then, but I know that I desperately wanted to. It was the only rational reason I could think of for the kind of life I was living at home. Believing that myth would have absolved me from a great deal of guilt.

Simply defined, the statement means that one can make up for having minimal moments with his family by making certain that the time he does have is quality time—fully devoted to the family with no secondary competing influence. Does that sound reasonable?

On the surface, this concept seems to make a lot of sense. It is possible to spend much time with one's family that is seemingly meaningless. All of us experience times when we are at home physically but our minds are wandering miles away. I can remember days with the family that could have been "scratched" in terms of "quality." Problems I was experiencing at work had me so preoccupied I was useless as a family participant. It was like having one broken finger on a hand, useless to the other four because it is bound in a splint and bandages.

So what is the "quality time" myth? It's as phony as the fake diamond in a one-dollar ring; it's the rationale that allows people like me to relieve a guilty conscience while we go on neglecting our responsibility as a parent. The fact is, there is no quality without quantity.

The fact is, there is no quality without quantity.

In studying the life of the great Old Testament personality, Abraham, we find he is one of the few characters in the Bible who illustrates the family life of his time. In the last days of the old patriarch, we are told about one of his final acts—one that brings me up short every time I read it. Before he died, Abraham "left everything he owned to Isaac" (Genesis 25:5). This statement describes what Abraham willed to his son . . . flocks, herds, servants, and wealth. However, I believe that Abraham gave Isaac much more than just material possessions. He left him the example of a life well lived. We may not be nearly as rich as Abraham in the way of worldly goods, and we certainly cannot bequeath what we do not have. But all of us will leave a legacy of values and principles which we have taught through our shared experiences and the daily examples of our lives.

Abraham's life was filled with the interaction of his family; his nomadic lifestyle demanded close family involvement. (It's difficult to be isolated while sharing a tent.) Isaac probably lived most of his young life in the daily presence of his father and during those years caught the beliefs of his dad and the convictions of his parents, not by structured teaching, but by everyday living. Isaac even reproduced some of Abraham's sins.

Abraham's greatest bequest to Isaac was not his vast wealth, but those spiritual priorities and convictions which were shaped in Isaac's life by daily communication between father and son.

BUT I'M NOT A SHEEPHERDER

No one is denying that times have changed. Most of us do not follow agricultural or rural lifestyles; our families have been decentralized by work, school, church, entertainment, and many other influences. We cannot restructure our society to promote more family togetherness, but neither can we pass our values on to our children unless we are willing to invest time in them.

Phillip Wylie observed there are 168 hours in the week. According to his analysis:

> The average man spends about 40 of them at work. Allow another 15 hours for commuting time, lunch, overtime, etc. Then set aside 56 hours, 8 each night, for sleep. That adds ups to 111 hours, leaving Dad 57 hours he can find time to be a father to his children. Now, how many of these does the average father actually spend with his children?
>
> One group of 300 seventh and eighth grade boys kept accurate records for a two-week period. The average time the father and son had alone together for an entire week was seven and one half minutes.[1]

Dr. James Dobson cites another study which concluded that the average middle-class father spent thirty-seven seconds per day with his small children. They had 2.7 encounters daily which lasted ten to fifteen seconds each.[2]

The total uninvolvement of her father prompted one precocious child to say, "Mommy, if the stork is supposed to bring babies, if Santa Claus brings presents, if the Lord gives us our daily bread and Uncle Sam our Social Security, why do we keep Daddy around?"

CAUSES OF THE ABSENTEE-PARENT FAMILY

During a panel discussion on "The Role of the Father in the Family," one of the participants asked how the present plight of the absentee-parent families had emerged. An important question. For no solutions can be offered for an illness until the causes are diagnosed. Many secondary forces might be cited, but I believe there are three basic influences eroding family life today. The first one may come as a shock to some of you.

1. *Religious Overcommitment.* If you are a Christian, you may have mentally advanced to the next chapter. Christians, especially the "deeply committed" variety, don't neglect their families. That's like accusing a surgeon of not washing his hands before an operation. However, overcommitment to the church is the number-one cause of family neglect among Christians; Dr. James Dobson believes it is the major marriage killer.

The insidious thing about overabundance of righteous activities is that you can neglect your family and feel extremely pious all the time you're doing it. After all, it's God's work.

One overcommitted Christian went to see his pastor one day about his runaway wife. "And when did she leave you?" the minister asked. "I'm not sure," said the layman. "It was sometime between Monday and Friday of this week. I've been at church every night, and I can't honestly say when it was."

If you're like me, just as a smile starts to form in response to that story, you swallow hard. There have been far too many weeks like that in my life.

2. *Workaholism.* A cartoon pictures a mother sitting on a shaggy rug with her little ones and explaining, "Your father, children, is six

feet tall, handsome, has a cute little mustache, is working like mad to
be the vice-president, and he simply loves golf."

Another vignette of the workaholic showed a big business executive in a waiting room on the maternity floor of the hospital. While
other expectant fathers paced the floor and thumbed nervously
through magazines, he sat at a table working furiously on a sheaf of
papers he had taken from his bulging briefcase.

After some hours, a nurse came into the room and spoke to him.
"It's a boy, sir," she said.

"Well," snapped the executive without looking up from his work,
"ask him what he wants."

It's no secret that for many modern men the excitement of management and leadership decisions makes home life seem dull. With
good mental intentions for the family, these executives allow themselves to be talked into attending this meeting, speaking at that
dinner, and helping with a "crucial" project. Their calendars fill up
months in advance, and what seemed like an innocent commitment
eighteen months ago to write or speak or participate in a meeting,
suddenly is eating away large chunks of time that belong to the
family.

Perhaps you've heard the song entitled "Cat's in the Cradle." It
graphically describes a father who cares deeply for his son, but is
just too busy becoming a business success to spend much time
with him. The years pass, and now the retired father has time, but
the grown son has become just like his dad: too busy making his
own success in life to take time out to be with his father.

When children grow up in a home with workaholic parents, they
get a badly warped view of family life. Two third-graders were
talking about their fathers. Catherine was frowning when she said,
"I hardly ever see my dad. It should be a law that all kids can see
their fathers. Mine works late and he's s'posed to be home Sundays,
but sometimes he works then, too."

Alan replied, "Well, if a man plays too much with his children,
he turns poor!"

The obvious value that is being taught to Catherine and Alan is
the mutual exclusiveness of business success and home life. Those
kids think you can't have one without giving up the other.

Many workaholic fathers have convinced themselves that they
are sacrificing for the future of their families, but the plain and
simple truth is this: workaholism is the epitome of selfishness.

The workaholic labors because his work meets his own needs; whether he knows it or not, he is meeting those needs at the expense of his family.

The Scriptures record the words of the great apostle Paul to the effect that a man who does not meet the needs of his family is worse than a pagan (1 Timothy 5:8). In reading this passage we might believe that Paul's primary focus is on the provision of food, shelter, and clothing. But I believe God holds the Christian father equally responsible for those needs which can only be met by his ongoing personal involvement with his family.

If you happen to be a workaholic, it's time to assume total responsibility for your life. If you are working too much at the expense of your family's well-being, it's not the company's fault. You don't have to play any success game you don't want to play. If you work too much, it's because you want to.

It's time to get honest about our habits. We don't need any more seminars in time management; we need to start talking about self-management. No matter what we do, time marches on consistently; it cannot be managed. *We need to manage ourselves.* Just being willing to understand that concept is a step in the right direction.

3. *Working Mothers.* According to surveys, in 1970 most married households were supported by a single wage earner. By 1980, more than half of all married households had two wage earners. By 1990, it is expected the number will rise to 80 percent.

Pressured by inflation and lured by the promise of fulfillment, women are leaving the home in droves. A growing number of children are being left to grow up alone without father or mother.

Dennis Agajanian, a gospel singer who attends our church, wrote and recorded a folk tune that describes the emptiness so many children feel because of absentee parents. He captures the emotion of the child in his song called "Child Cry."

Where you been? Are you hidin'?
Where can they be? Why am I cryin'?
Is the future more than me?
Nobody's home.

Come home from school, it's cold and rainin',
Wish there were cookies Mom was bakin',
This day-care center's not for me,
Nobody's home.

A child cries for parents, a times a changin',
Is the future worth it all?
Makin' lots of money, for Daddy's car, Mom's home,
No one's ever here and I'm alone.

Look out the window, see Mom comin'
I'll wash my tears, she'll wonder why I'm cryin',
Play like I've had lots of fun, that I didn't get scared,
I'm scared . . .

Where ya been? Are you hidin'?
Where can they be? Why am I cryin'?
Is the future more than me?
Nobody's home, no one's ever home.[3]

Some women have no choice; many single mothers would love to be able to stay home with their children, but must work to provide for their needs. I really believe God can work family miracles for those who honestly have no alternative in this matter.

Being a mother is a demanding, frustrating, but completely fulfilling and rewarding career. In *A Man Called Peter,* Catherine Marshall told how her late husband tended to put women on a pedestal. She quoted the following from one of his sermons:

Modern gals argue that they have to earn income in order to establish a home, which would be impossible on their husband's income. That is sometimes the case, but it must always be viewed as a regrettable necessity, never as the normal or natural thing for a wife to have to do. The average woman, if she gives her full time to her home, her husband, her children . . . if she tries to understand her husband's work . . . to curb his egotism, at the same time building up his self-esteem, to kill his masculine conceit, while, at the same time, encouraging all his hopes, to establish around the family a circle of true friends . . . if she provides in the home a proper atmosphere of culture, . . . if she can do all this, she will be engaged in a life work that will demand every ounce of strength, every bit of her patience, every talent God has given her, the utmost sacrifice of her love. It will demand everything she has and more. And she will find that for which she was created. She will know that she is carrying out the plan of God. She will be partner with the Sovereign Ruler of the universe.[4]

I believe that represents the biblical ethic for women. I know many women today have to discard the ideal in order to cope with reality, and I do not say that is wrong. However, there is no way for mothers or fathers to trade off their time for material possessions. If the truth were known, most of our children would give back the junk we purchased with our overtime hours just to have spent more time with us. The mother of three boys wrote: "I realize now that there will never be another time when I can observe so closely the mysterious and unpredictable changes as little boys grow up. I'm glad I'm able to be around so much to watch, for mixed with the annoyances and the frustrations of the 'quantity time' I spend with my charges are moments of pure quality that surprise and exhilarate."[5]

BUILDING SPECIAL TIMES

One of the happy thoughts of my growing-up days is the memory of my mother's consistent support of all my school activities, whether it was a basketball game, a track meet, or a school play. Dad came to most of these events, as his schedule would allow, but Mom never missed. I remember vividly running out on the court for a basketball game and scanning the crowd until I saw Mom. Before the night was over, I usually heard her, too. She was one of our most vocal fans.

In a very special way, my dad has participated in every major event in my life. He gave the baccalaureate address when I graduated from high school, handed me my diploma when I graduated from college, pronounced Donna and me man and wife, took part in my senior chapel in seminary, and preached my ordination sermon. Those times were very special for both of us. Obviously, my opportunity was unique as the son of a Christian leader, but I know that Mom and Dad would have been present for all those events, even if they had not participated.

As parents, Donna and I have adopted a similar habit; and with four children, believe me, it's a challenge. As soon as the school drama and athletic schedules are printed, we get them to my secretary, and she puts them on my calendar. Sometimes we feel very strange about our commitment. To say "Sorry, I can't speak for your meeting, because my son has a basketball game" sounds like a feeble excuse to some.

One year I coached our son's Little League team, and I was disturbed by the lack of support and interest on the part of most parents. Some of the boys on our team never had the privilege of playing one game in front of their parents all year.

There are some things in the lives of our children we dare not miss. You can call it quality or quantity, but we had better be there!

Spontaneous time can't be scheduled.

Spontaneous time can't be scheduled. One of the serious flaws in the "quality time" myth is its inability to deal with those sudden bursts of communication or events of family life that occur unexpectedly. I never cease to be amazed at the way children can turn their communication "circuits" on and off without provocation. Our two oldest children can sometimes go for what seems like days without communicating anything about their lives. Then, all of a sudden, for a reason I seldom understand, they decide to tell it all. How important it is for someone to be there at those special times to listen.

I remember the time Jan came home from a church youth group party called "Mission Impossible." As soon as I came into the room, she began to rattle off the endless details of her evening, who she was with, where they went, how scared she was (about every other breath), how neat it was, how much fun she had. All the minutiae stretched to the outer limits of description.

I kept thinking, *Get on with it . . . good grief, Jan, hurry up; I could have said that in one-tenth of the time.* My facial expressions and body language must have communicated to her exactly what I was thinking. But at the moment those events were very important in her life.

Looking back on that experience, and others like it, I realize that I often rudely cut off the conversation, even by walking away. I am beginning to learn that those times are precious and to be thankful for the privilege of being there when special moments occur. It won't be long until our children will be in their next stage of life, and we will be begging for any scrap of information we can glean from their busy, private lives.

Gloria Gaither had these spontaneous moments in mind when she wrote the lyrics of "We Have This Moment Today."

Hold tight to the sound of the music of living,
Happy songs from the laughter of children at play;
Hold my hand as we run through the sweet fragrant meadows.
Making memories of what was today.

Tiny voice that I hear is my little girl calling,
For Daddy to hear just what she has to say;
My little son running there by the hillside,
May never be quite like today.

We have this moment to hold in our hand,
And to touch as it slips through our fingers like sand.
Yesterday's gone and tomorrow may never come,
But we have this moment today.

IF ONLY . . .

Too many parents live with the regrets of abandoned moments. It takes time to be silly, to share a secret, to heal a hurt, to kiss away a tear. Moments of uninhibited communication between child and parent cannot be planned; they just happen. The only ingredient we bring to that dynamic of family life is our availability . . . and that is spelled T-I-M-E.

A young couple we know are extremely busy and talented. He is a doctor with a demanding practice; she is the head of a crisis counseling center. Both are in demand for their singing abilities. After a particularly busy day, Teri was putting their two young children to bed and was convicted, as we all are at times, about the amount of time she and Paul had been devoting to their family. She wrote this song:

It's nine-fifteen and bedtime took too long (once again)
Another kiss, another glass of water, and then
The questions come . . . the hands hold tight . . . the eyes are open wide
And something in me whispers, "Now's the time . . ."

"Mommy, why did Muffy die?" "Daddy, where's the sun?"
"Are there cats in heaven?" and "Why did Jesus come?"
And though a whole day's dishes wait, and bills are piled high,
Something in me whispers . . . "Take the time . . ."

CHORUS:
  Take the time while they're right here by your side
  Take the time while their hearts are open wide
Teach them how to love the Lord with all their hearts and minds.
  Oh, they're only home a season . . . take the time![7]

Soon after we moved to California, I was invited to lunch by one of the fathers in our church. As we ate, he shared the story of the tragic death of his son. He was a handsome junior in our Christian High School, a promising athlete and a fine young man. He was riding in the back of a friend's van when the vehicle was run off the road and a big three-wheeled ATV, which was being transported in the van, fell over on him, crushing him to death.

As Stan told me of this experience and the tremendous spiritual struggle he had undergone since then, he included a report of an encounter he had had with another father who also had lost his grown son through an accident. As the two had conversed, the other father asked Stan this penetrating question: "If you could, would you give everything you own to spend just one day with your boy?" Stan had been a faithful father and had given a great deal of time to his son, but without hesitation, he said, "Yes."

Given the same question, in the same set of circumstances, all of us would no doubt have responded as Stan did.

What is tragic is that while we would gladly sacrifice everything for the unobtainable, we give up almost nothing for that which is available to us upon request.

This is the myth: "It's not the quantity of time you spend with your children, but the quality of time." We are always struggling with demands for our time: job, church activities, club work, social obligations, educational pursuits, recreational needs, and desires. We run through life breathless and stop exhausted. But among our top priorities is to try to be there during those *special times* in our family's life; to plan to use *scheduled times* when our children are involved in their activities; to be available for *spontaneous times* which occur at the most unexpected moments. Those are the quality times of life to cherish in our memory albums of our children's growing up.

I think the unknown writer of these simple lines was trying to communicate the truth of our quality/quantity time myth.

What shall you give to one small boy?
A glamorous game, a tinseled toy,
A barlow knife, a puzzle pack,
A train that runs on curving track?
A picture book, a real live pet . . .
No, there's plenty of time for such things yet.

Give him a day for his very own,
Just one small boy and his Dad alone,
A walk in the woods, a romp in the park,
A fishing trip from dawn to dark,
Give him the gift that only you have,
The companionship of his dear Dad.

Games are outgrown and toys decay,
But he'll never forget if you give him a day.

If I've learned one thing during these days of growing family awareness in my life, it's been this: there are others who can counsel, others who can make personnel decisions, others who can administrate the organization, but there is only one man in the whole world who can be a father to my children—and that's me! I had better be that father while I have the opportunity.

MYTH THREE

She's Mommy's Girl

*S*he sat in my office, a dejected, frightened, angry young lady. As she stared at the floor and poured out her story, it was one which could be duplicated across the country. Her trembling voice was almost a whisper as she told me, "I can't remember one time when my father put his arms around me and said, 'I love you.' So I went out and found the best kind of love I could find."

Those tear-choked words from an unmarried, pregnant teenager triggered a process in my own mind which is responsible, more than anything else, for this book.

Was this troubled girl just dumping her problems on her father— or was she verbalizing for a generation of women a real and significant truth? That evening I arrived home from my office with the desire to reach out and hug my two daughters as they had never been hugged before.

As I shared this little episode with friends and colleagues, I found there was consistent support for the discovery I was making. *Many fathers do not have a close relationship with their daughters, and most don't think it vitally important.* After all, the reasoning goes, "Dads are for sons and Moms are for daughters." Is that statement completely true? I believe "She's Mommy's Girl" is a myth which implies that Daddy's influence is low in priority. In reality, the most important relationship within the family, second only to that of husband and wife, is the relationship between father and daughter.

In *Fathers and Daughters*, Dr. William S. Appleton wrote, "For any woman, one very dominating influence is her father. He is the first man to whom she gives her heart, and how he reacts strongly affects her future with men."[1]

WHAT ARE FATHERS FOR?

A girl's father is the first man in her life, and probably the most influential. Absent or involved, loving or rejecting, what he is or was leaves a lasting imprint. Most women have not analyzed their relationships with their fathers, and until recently the father-daughter bond has not received the spotlight it deserves. A woman may speak of her father with pride or revulsion, she may compare him favorably or unfavorably to the other men in her life. But whatever life with father has been, a father's role sets the stage for a woman's performance.

> A girl's father is the first man in her life, and probably the most influential. Absent or involved, loving or rejecting, what he is or was leaves a lasting imprint.

Corrie ten Boom wove many of her life's experiences around her father, Casper ten Boom, a humble watchmaker in Haarlem, Holland. Thus the story of his witness for the Lord was spread around the world. On the other hand, we don't have to go far to hear the cries of father-haters or the complaints of father-accusers. Some women blame their fathers for their own mistakes or shortcomings; today a juicy revelation about good old Dad may even end up on the best-seller list.

It's not easy to define fatherhood in our society, because the roles of men and women have changed so that *parenting* and *parenthood* are androgynous terms. A few generations ago the duties and obligations were more clearly defined: father brought home the bacon and mother cooked it. This generation of kids has grown up in a changing society that accepts women who work outside of the home and men who do household chores; children don't think this is unusual, as long as their basic needs are met. But if women can do the jobs previously done by men, what purpose does father have?

In a two-parent family, the father should provide the bulk of the family income. The Bible says: "But if any one does not provide for his own, and especially for those of his household, he has denied the faith, and is worse than an unbeliever" (1 Timothy 5:8, NASB).

However, to be a *breadwinner* is more than just putting food on the table and a new car in the garage. It's providing the little treats a child will cherish long after the mortgage is paid. Though I am not a wealthy man in terms of the American standard, one of my secret joys is giving my kids the small extras. For instance, we have some silly Sunday rituals with our children. Between church services I go into my study to prepare myself for the next hour, and within a short time I can expect our two youngest, Daniel and Jennifer, to come in with those hungry looks on their faces. I give them some change to get a treat from a little place on our campus, and they run out quickly to make it back before the next hour begins. It would have been just as easy to give them some money before that time, but it would have taken a little fun out of the morning. When Jan was home, she would go through the receiving line after the evening service, and I made a point of greeting her formally, "Hello, young lady, I'm so glad you came this evening." She might say, "Oh, Daddy, cut it out. I just wanted to ask you if it is okay to go out for ice cream with the gang." I'd usually say, "Sure," and then turn to greet the next person. Jan would tug on my sleeve, and I'd say, as if it never occurred to me before, "Oh, do you need some money?" Of course these episodes are just a part of family trivia, but they're fun—and the kids started to call me Daddy Deep-Pockets.

Fathers are for financial support, but they're also to be a comforter in time of need. One woman told me her first childhood memory was of her father holding her and walking the floor after she had had a bad fall. She said, "I can still feel his big shoulder and smell the cigars on his clothes. To this day I think of that time whenever I smell cigars." One of the closest bonds a father can have with his daughter comes through comforting.

A father also is for understanding. That's a tough one, because more often we dads say, "I just don't understand her!" Perhaps it's because we haven't tried to understand. I admit, a girl isn't easy to figure out; she's a miniature woman, and no man alive would dare say he understood women. As soon as he made that presumptuous statement he would be branded a liar! I would like to meet the father who hasn't heard, "But, Dad, you don't understand." Daughters seem to use that phrase more often than sons; for a few years, usually between the ages of twelve and eighteen, those words are a familiar theme.

That celebrity father, Bill Cosby, wrote:

> A famous actor with two daughters once told me, "When a girl
> hits thirteen, you can just watch her lose her mind. Luckily, she gets
> it back; but during all the time that it's misplaced, you can lose your
> own."
>
> In these trying years, as I have said, and can't say too often, a
> father just has to keep hanging around and loving and knowing that
> his baby needs guidance because her own rudder hasn't started
> working yet. To extend the nautical image, a father during these
> years has to do everything in his power to keep a tight ship, even
> though he knows the crew would like to send him away in a dinghy.[2]

Solomon wasn't called the wisest man for nothing. The Book of
Proverbs is better than any self-appointed child expert. "He who
restrains his words has knowledge, and he who has a cool spirit is a
man of understanding" (Proverbs 17:27, NASB).

And you probably thought the word *cool* was coined by a rock
musician. Surprise! It was King David's son, three thousand years
ago. The important thing here is when it comes to understanding,
we fathers need to listen first to the explanations and then stay
cool.

Fathers are for fun. I've seen fathers who are so reserved
around their daughters that I've wanted to let the air out of their
inflated balloons. Or else Dad is that remote individual who ap-
pears (sometimes) for meals, then hurries off to meetings. He may
be present for the prescribed times of fun during annual vacations,
but on a day-to-day basis, he's as bland as sugarless vanilla pud-
ding. After the stage of playing horsey on the floor has passed, he
forgets that his girls will absorb his sense of humor just as much as
his moral values and standards.

Fathers should be confidence builders. "Fathers are as important as mothers in making girls comfortable and confident. If a
father rejects what a girl feels is important to her sense of herself,
or makes fun of it or disapproves, it's trouble."[3]

Comfort . . . confidence . . . acceptance—they're all part of
the same parcel we dads should give to our daughters. Of course,
we don't want to accept behavior which is immoral, dangerous, or
senseless. But we must make sure that our daughters know that we
always love and accept them. One successful young businesswoman
told me that after her father and mother divorced she lived with her

father from the time she was six until she was fifteen. Her father was very strict, and in his anxiety to be a good father, he tried to mold her into his concept of a perfect "little lady." He constantly criticized her, without offering encouragement. "All I wanted to hear was 'I'm really proud of you,'" she said. She added fuel to her father's disapproval by dating men much older than she. When she was sixteen she was going with a fellow who was twenty-eight, and by the time she was twenty her steady boyfriend was a man of thirty-eight, only two years younger than her dad.

Fathers are for role models. It's a scary thing to realize that *what we are* affects our children more than *what we say*. Daughters will perceive how women should be treated (or not treated) according to how Dad treats Mother and other women. A girl gets the picture of what to be from the way she sees her father react to women in general and to her in particular. The days of sharply defined roles for men and women are long gone. A father may be a career model for his daughter, something which was exceptional in past generations. The popular adage "like father, like son" implies that sons are more like their dads in personality traits. That is not always true. A girl may be a great deal like her father, especially if he spends much time with her. In an article on "How Fathers Influence Daughters," Dr. Alexandra Symons, associate clinical professor of psychiatry at the New York University School of Medicine, made a study of women who had high commitments to work. "Most of the studies show that the highest percentage of women who aspire to careers have been encouraged or influenced by men, their fathers, usually," she said.[4]

We fathers are very important in our daughters' lives. And I think when we see what a good father means to a girl, it makes it easier to be one.

FAMOUS FATHERS AND THEIR DAUGHTERS

Winston Churchill's daughter wrote:

> The greatest and most powerful influence in my early life was, of course, my father. Although I had talked with him so seldom and never for a moment on equal terms, I conceived an intense admiration and affection for him; and after his death, for his memory. I

read industriously almost every word he had ever spoken and
learned by heart large portions of his speeches . . . . He seemed
to own the key to everything or almost everything worth having.[5]

Another twentieth century leader was Jawaharlal Nehru. His
daughter, Indira Gandhi, became Prime Minister of India, the
world's largest democracy and the country with the second largest
population; she has been regarded as one of the outstanding
women of this century. Although both parents were strong examples of intense loyalty to their motherland, it was her father's influence that formed the pattern for her life as a leader. He took a
keen interest in her education and encouraged her to read and
think for herself. While he was away, he carried on a great dia-
logue with her through letters. Later these letters were published
in a book.

One of the most poignant stories about Indira Gandhi was related
after she married and had a son. Her father had been arrested and
was to be transferred from one prison to another. Indira's baby was
only a few months old and his grandfather had never seen him. She
learned that the route the car bearing her father would take was
over a certain bridge. At dusk, wearing a sari which her father had
woven for her, she stood in a visible spot near the bridge and lifted
the baby high above her head so that Nehru could catch a glimpse of
his grandchild.

When India became independent and Nehru was elected as
Prime Minister, Indira served as his hostess and later participated
in policy making and vital decisions. Her father wove more than a
sari for her; he designed the fabric of her life.

IS DAD REALLY THAT IMPORTANT?

The American father does not have a family crest, a title, tribal
authority, or a patriarchal stance. When "Faith of Our Fathers"
is sung, it may be impossible for most people to determine what
that faith is. Many women keep their maiden names as a means of
personal identity. We may be a nation of self-made men, but in the
process we have become a nation where the great American insti-
tution is the almighty individual, not the strong father. One writer
for a scholarly journal said, "As social welfare undertakes the

material responsibilities for child care, the old necessity for fathers is considerably weakened."[6]

Now wait a minute! Fathers *are* important! A daughter may model herself after and identify with her mother in many ways, but she learns about men, for better or worse, from her father.

I am deeply concerned about the role of the father in our American culture today. The attempts on the part of the media to downgrade his influence, along with the feminist attack on his importance and worth, are the ingredients which are contributing to the weakening of our country. Men have become feminized and modern women have been masculinized. If we are to regain leadership among the nations of the earth, men must become men again.

Yes, Dad, you are exceedingly important. You touch the life of your daughter in many ways. Until recently, few people have given the father-daughter bond the attention it deserves. We need to turn the spotlight on and see how dads affect their girls.

For one thing, fathers affect the *self-esteem* of their daughters. Most men probably don't realize that the words they use or don't use, the looks they give or don't give, can be crucial in a girl's view of herself. Sincere compliments, frequently given, are like fudge to a chocoholic. As a teenager, Connie was at the top of her class in grades. She was frequently told by her mother, "Honey, you'll never be real pretty, but you certainly will go a long way with your mind." At the age of fourteen, a girl is not as interested in her intellectual prowess as in her physical impression. Connie told me this story many years after the fact as she shared these positive words her father said to her: "Honey, please don't stop smiling, because you have the prettiest smile of anyone I know." What do you think she did around her father? Of course, she smiled. Her dad constantly reinforced her as being a pretty girl. He was wise enough to realize appearance was her greatest struggle at a time when looks seem so important.

Self-esteem has to be taught because others want to destroy it. Preadolescent and adolescent girls have a certain destructive power all their own when it comes to tearing away at their own image or that of the girl down the street. Someone else's daughter is considered cruel when her barbs are aimed at your offspring, but the subtle cruelty fathers can inflict on their own daughters may produce hidden scars which are far more painful.

In a story for *McCall's* magazine, Phyllis Theroux tells about herself as a preteen who had just moved to a new neighborhood that was as lonely as the adolescence she was entering. She compensated for her misery by eating ice cream cones and candy bars in hidden binges. Her father called her his "fat fairy," an endearment that was not dear to her. She staged hunger strikes, locking herself in her room during the day and sneaking down to the kitchen to devour a loaf of Wonder Bread at night. As the fat accumulated, so did her misery.

In the middle of her sixth-grade year, invitations were sent out for a formal Father-Daughter dance at the school she attended. Her mother got a special dress "worn only twice" from her cousin Mimi. As Phyllis looked at the limp, uninspiring dress, which accentuated her pudgy frame, she decided she didn't want to go to the dance at all. However, from a wise and repentant father came a present she never forgot. He took the day off work and traipsed in and out of unfamiliar department stores to find two dresses he thought might be right. Phyllis said, "I cannot think about what those boxes contained without feeling the same disbelief that overcame me then. I opened the first and out sprang a pink net formal, covered with tiny stars. Out of the second box came a pale-blue net dress with white daisies embroidered all over the full skirt. Suddenly the room was full of white tissue and hope."

Years later Phyllis's tender story, *The Father-Daughter Dance*, is a tribute to what a father can do to a little girl's self-esteem with one simple gesture. She says:

> He was, of course, the handsomest without doubt, and the first prince in my life to come through, unwittingly setting me up for every other prince who was delayed in transit later on . . . . One night does not melt away adolescence, but I'm glad I have it to look back to. It confirms my deepest feelings about my father, who confirmed my deepest hopes for myself. The night was full of light, contentment and store-bought stars, and I don't know how to repay my father for it except to tell the story and let it stand on its own—like a new dress.[7]

I think Phyllis repaid her father, don't you?

When a girl is at the adolescent stage of life, a father's occupation and social class may have a strong effect on her self-esteem. One university-educated career woman told me how she can remember her acute embarrassment with her father's poor use of English when he visited her junior high teacher. Her dad was not an educated man, but he had one of the most flourishing businesses in their small town. However, as his daughter grew up and recognized his accomplishments, she realized that she had learned more about ethics, integrity, and personal drive from her father than she ever learned in college. I'm convinced that most daughters would like to disown their fathers at some time in their lives, and allow us to reestablish our paternal rights when we are no longer a threat to their reputation.

A father affects his daughter's *choice of a husband*. Looking at my two girls, and realizing that they may be attracted to a man who emulates my qualities, drives me to my knees. I read studies by clinical psychologists who have said that a woman who has a deep, positive experience with her father is likely to pick a mate just like him. That knowledge in itself should motivate us men to follow the admonitions of Paul when he must have looked some of the men of the city of Corinth in the eyes and said, "Check up on yourselves. Are you really Christians? Do you pass the test? Do you feel Christ's presence and power more and more within you? Or are you just pretending to be Christians when actually you aren't at all?" (2 Corinthians 13:5, TLB). I know I am a Christian, but I desire with all my heart to feel Christ's presence and power. If there's a chance that my daughters will choose a mate with any of my qualities, I hope it will be because I've provided a decent role model.

A father may affect his daughter's *career direction*. Whether he approves or disapproves, a girl may find herself strongly influenced by what her father thinks. If he's the type of man who says, "Honey, I'll support your decision, no matter what it is," and their relationship has been close, a girl will experience the freedom she wants, with the security she needs. Too many times, however, her aspirations and Dad's ambitions may clash. Probably some of the most degrading words he could use would be, "What on earth do you want to do that for?" Or, "Are you kidding? You mean you want to go *there?*"

The president of Radcliffe, Matina Horner, made a study of women's fear of success. She concluded that in the majority of young women who feared success, most came from upper-middle-class and middle-class homes, where their fathers were successful business and professional men.[8]

One of the great challenges fathers face, especially if they have sons, too, is to find the balance in relationship with their girls. Since I am athletically inclined, and my boys are very involved with team sports, I have had to make a real effort to do things with Jan that she enjoys. When she went to school in the Dominican Republic, I flew down with her. When she returned to the States via Miami, I met her and came back to California with her. Jan was seventeen at the time and perfectly capable of traveling on her own, but I wanted her to know that I was by her side and an ally, not an adversary. This may have nothing to do with influencing her career, but I want her to know that I support her.

On the trip to the Dominican Republic, when Jan went away to school for the first time, we were both so tense that everything was magnified into far more importance than it might normally have been. We got lost in Santa Domingo and found ourselves in the produce section where all the trucks were loading and unloading. There was no place to turn around; we didn't know the language, so we couldn't ask directions. In the Dominican Republic there seems to be no order to the traffic, and we were completely confused when a truck ran into our rental car and put a large dent in the side. I tried to call the police, but they don't bother to come to accidents in Santa Domingo. By this time Jan was in tears, totally frustrated with me and upset because we were going to be late and she wouldn't see the one friend she knew who was already in the school.

As we look back on that intense period of time, we just crack up. Here we were together in one of the most important experiences of her life and everything seemed to go wrong. However, it's these very memories that are now precious to us.

Through the years Jan and I have had difficulty finding common interests, but before she went away to school we tried to coordinate our schedules so we could go to breakfast on Saturday mornings. I tried to pick very special places, restaurants where we would not normally eat an evening meal because they were too expensive. But for breakfast, we could be extravagant. Those times were very special.

Jan and I have had a different relationship from the one Jennifer and I have. When Jan was between the second grade and high school, I never felt very close to her; she was on her own journey, and it didn't include me. I'm not saying that it doesn't take two to make the trip, because I was more at fault than she. Jennifer, on the other hand, is our third child; she has had the advantage of the more relaxed upbringing. And I have learned to loosen up and laugh at the inconveniences of fatherhood.

Monday is the one night of the week during the fall that I unashamedly devote to television viewing. You guessed it; I'm a Monday night football fan. It was on one of these evenings that Jennifer chose to ask for "just a little favor." She was campaigning for class secretary, and she and Donna had found some little cardboard rings to use as publicity giveaways. Donna told Jennifer I was good at printing (although I'm not sure where she got that idea), and so I ended up printing "Jennifer for Secretary" a hundred times on those little rings. I lost track of most of the game as a consequence, and I worked very late on my campaign contribution. The next night Jennifer returned and said, "Dad, the rings are all gone. Will you print some more for me?" My profession had been chosen. Perhaps I could try the Lord's prayer on the head of a pin next.

It's a shame that a first child has to live with the inexperience of his or her parents. But somehow these first-born survive and grow, in spite of us.

FATHER/DAUGHTER STAGES

Father/daughter experiences progress through stages; the closeness we fathers feel will vary with the ages of our girls. During their children's *infancy* stage, more of the younger fathers today bathe, feed, and change diapers, either because it's more acceptable or they are sharing some of the child-raising and housework with their wives. I must admit I hated changing diapers; I didn't want any part of it. But I can remember walking the floor with Jan from ten at night until two in the morning because she had colic. In our first house, our kitchen, dining room, and living room were joined together in a circle. I did laps around those rooms until I knew exactly how many steps there were and where the floor board creaked. Some things you never forget. With the rest of the kids, we did our share of floor walking, but we weren't so tense. Experience is a great relaxer.

There's something very special about a loving father and his infant daughter. He takes her to the market even when he hates to grocery shop. He makes silly faces and uses language in an alien tongue. His voice goes up an octave, and he throws a burping cloth over his best blue suit, leaving lint particles clinging to his shoulder. He makes an utter fool of himself, and no one cares.

I suppose clinical studies on parent-child relationships have their place in our understanding, although I'm not sure what they accomplish, except to show some of us we are normal when we were beginning to think no one else ever thought the way we did. One researcher made a study of how much time fathers spend in vocal interaction with their infant daughters. It was shown that the fathers in the test cases vocalized to their girl babies about thirty seconds a day.[9]

It's a wonder a baby girl doesn't cry more around Daddy; he talks to her so seldom that when he does, she doesn't recognize his voice.

However, younger fathers today have moved with the times. They tend to a small child's physical needs more than their fathers did, and, in most cases, considerably more than their grandfathers. Beyond the physical caretaking, there is not much difference between the dads of today and the fathers of yesterday. One of my unscientific, unprovable theories is that more fathers of this generation help with the diaper-changing routine because disposable diapers make it so much easier—they were designed for the most awkward bumbler to use. Don't quote me, though.

During *childhood* a daughter may idealize her father. Suzanne Fields tells about the time when she was five and "married" her dad in a mock ceremony, wearing her best party dress and a pink corsage, attended by her mother as "matron of honor" and brother as "rabbi." Fields said that after she started school and her world expanded beyond the house where Daddy lived, she grew shy and was embarrassed about the "wedding."[10]

In most cases, the childhood stage occurs during the period when the father is in his thirties. It's a time when Dad is usually preoccupied with career at the expense of his marriage, his friendships, his leisure, and his attention to his children. During this time, his daughter may not see a lot of him, but when he is there, away from the hard, competitive world, it's what Dr. Appleton in *Fathers and Daughters* calls the "oasis period." His little girl may be the diversion and rest from the heat of his job or career. Of course, if his tired wife calls upon him for complete child care, what may have been a delight turns into a burden.

We dads should never get the impression that our wives are the ones who are the most important persons in forming the future of our daughters. The legacy we leave from the investment in that first decade of their lives can be a lasting one.

> The way a father treats his daughter in the oasis period makes an indelible impression on her. By overdoing it he may cause her to long all her life for this time when she was the center of his attention . . . . If there was no happiness or too little with her father in the oasis period, a girl's femininity suffers. Their first decade together not only includes her need to form an infant's attachment but if the father is absent or angry and rejecting, leaves the girl completely discouraged in her beginning and most important efforts with a man. . . . It is surprising that fathers affect their daughters' femininity more than their sons' masculinity.[11]

For many little girls, life with father is a dress rehearsal for love and marriage. Feelings are so intense during childhood that most people can vividly remember vignettes from their early years, while recent events may be obscure. Kay recalls the night some businessmen were at their house and her father excused himself and went into her room to read her a story and hear her prayers. Pamela remembers the overnight camping trip with her dad when a fierce crack of thunder made her awaken with a scream and her father said, "It's okay, honey, Daddy's here." She said that in later life she could relate to a Father-God who assured her, "Don't be afraid, I'm with you always."

For many little girls, life with father is a dress rehearsal for love and marriage.

Some sociologists see women in two basic categories: Daddy's girls and Mother's daughters. The child identifies with one as her hero or heroine; the other parent is less important. Daddy's girl discovers at a very early age the power she holds over men. She can "wrap him around her little finger." Mommy's girl is more inclined

to get along better with women, take her mother's side in any arguments with Dad, and doesn't expect much from men. The way a
father treats his daughter during this childhood period makes
a lasting impression upon her. If Dad is attentive, loving, but firm,
she has more of a chance of entering the turbulent teens with a
great sense of security. On the other hand, an absent, withdrawn, or
rejecting father may cause that girl to feel insecure about herself,
her attractiveness, or acceptance by the opposite sex.

Studies have been made which indicate that fathers of children
five to twelve years old reward their daughters only about half as
much as their sons when they are well behaved.[12] When I read that,
I thought of the verse which says, "Fathers, don't scold your children so much that they become discouraged and quit trying"
(Colossians 3:21, TLB). But, dads, in the same manner, don't play
favorites with praise and rewards, lest your little girl becomes discouraged and quits trying. We all flourish on encouragement and
wilt with criticism.

One woman told me that as a child her greatest desire for achievement came as a result of wanting to make her father proud of her.
For little girls, Daddy's praise seems to mean more than Mom's.

Perhaps some women might stop at this point and begin to
point the finger of blame at what their father did (or did not do)
during their childhood. "If my father had paid more attention to
me I wouldn't be such a demanding wife." Or, "I was so spoiled
by my father that I have expected every man to treat me the same
way." Effects of early childhood relationships can be undone.
The woman who continues to fix the blame for her adult behavior
on her father's behavior toward her in the first decade of her life
is ignoring the fact that we have responsibility for our own lives as
adults. The Scriptures say: "When I was a child, I talked like a
child, I thought like a child, I reasoned like a child. When I
became a man [or woman], I put childish ways behind me" (1
Corinthians 13:11).

The next stage of father-daughter relationships is the *age of conflict*. I don't intend to speak something into existence, but when a
daughter is struggling from childhood to womanhood, her father
may be plowing through his own midlife crisis. She's trying to find
the answer to the universal cry of "Who am I?" while he is going
through a period in his life when he questions his career, his success
ratio, and his future direction. A father may be in between the end

of growing up and the beginning of growing old while his "little girl" is struggling to be "her own person."

The first conflict at this stage usually starts with appearance. Father's idea of proper, stylish attire may be as outmoded in his daughter's eyes as bustles. Daughter follows the crowd with whatever is "in" at the time, and poor Dad groans and makes subtle remarks like, "You're going to school in that? You've got to be kidding!" And his former little girl bristles like a startled porcupine. Authority meets stubbornness, and the winner loses the argument. Most fathers have said more than once, "You can't win!"

From clothes to make-up ("Wash your face, young lady!") to curfew hours and boyfriends, the age of conflict begins with small skirmishes and may develop into full-scale war if not halted. Those warm, positive feelings of childhood begin to slide as a girl discovers the growing world of temptation.

I have been asked if I taught my girls the facts of life. I suppose, in a limited way, that I have; but Donna has gone with the girls to a special course offered by the school. I have never felt a compulsion to sit down at a specific time and place and talk about sex with either of my girls; on the other hand, they have both heard me teach from the pulpit a positive view of sexual relations within marriage. They know that I think Victorian views on a subject which is treated by the Bible in such a positive manner are outmoded. Most of all, however, I have worked at developing an open-minded and loving relationship with each of my girls— one which I hope will lay a solid foundation for their later sexual attitudes, and consequently for their success with men throughout the rest of their lives. As one writer has said, "Girls who get on well with their fathers find marriage easier."[13] It's not difficult to see the domino effect on future marriages that may be caused by an ineffectual or absent father.

I believe some of the more dangerous attitudes of the feminist movement have been fostered by the weak fathers of America. A statement made by a woman writer was, "The decline of father may well be the best thing that has ever happened to girls. The current generation of feminist writers have found their voice partly because fathers have not been around in sufficient force to tell them that it might be unladylike to shout like that."[14] Dads, we might take a good look at ourselves before we begin to judge the political and social views of feminism.

LIKE FATHER/LIKE DAUGHTER

As more women step into the business and professional arena, fathers' influence is taking a new turn. Feminist author and founder of *MS.* magazine, Gloria Steinem, said, "Prefeminism, we used to treat fathers as though they were stars in the East. Now that we've established that children are not the sole responsibility of the mother, we're taking a closer look at the fathers."[15] More researchers are suggesting that men can provide a great boost to their daughters' professional success in a male-dominated world. San Francisco Mayor Dianne Feinstein said her father taught her how to deal with the intricacies of bureaucracies, and "Deep within him he believed that whatever I reached for was attainable, while I did not always believe it was."[16]

Cable-TV reporter Cissy Baker remembers how her father, Presidential Assistant Howard Baker, would catch a plane from Washington at 3 A.M., just so he could be home when she got up. Cheryl Miller, the most heavily recruited female athlete in history, told how her father, former All-American Saul Miller, coached her on their backyard basketball court from the time she was five. Women of great achievement, such as Virginia Woolf, Madame Curie, and Indira Gandhi, were partly raised and educated by encouraging fathers. A Los Angeles career consultant, Adele Scheele, said, "Fathers make fabulous mentors . . . the best."[17]

As encouraging as these examples may seem, the feminists do not seem to be satisfied with our performance, dads. The fathers who provide career models are said to be the exception. We are told, "By and large the centuries of patriarchy, of a world run by fathers, have been centuries that have put women down. Today the feminist press is busy publishing details of these long years of paternal blight. While inspiring their sons to aim for the stars, fathers have reared their daughters just to fit in."[18]

I must admit it's difficult for me to swallow the idea that there have been "long years of paternal blight," when the current generation has seen more fathers who have abandoned their responsibilities in pursuit of their own pleasures. However, I do believe that in this era when our girls may pursue careers their grandmothers would have labeled "men's work," fathers can have a profound and positive influence by providing guidance and encouragement.

A father shouldn't want to clone his daughter any more than his son. If my daughters go into Christian work, that's fine; however, my greatest desire is for their happiness in knowing that they are in God's will in their choice of career and/or mate. I believe there is a strong movement in America to drive a wedge between father-daughter, husband-wife, man-woman relationships—the very foundation of family life in our country. Those voices are strong enough to be featured by *Time* magazine in the cover article, "Are Women Fed Up?" Cited is a voluminous report by a leading feminist, which, according to the *Time* article, "so resonates with angry voices that the volume fairly vibrates in one's hand. . . . Hardest to swallow is the unrelieved bitterness and rage against men expressed throughout the report's pages."[19]

The wedge is being driven into our relationships, and it is up to us as parents to counteract with positive action.

WHO MAKES THE BEST DAD?

Kids probably think of Daddy Warbucks, giving Annie everything her heart desires, as the ideal father. Going from a poor little orphan to a girl with clothes, servants, and private showings of first-run movies may sound like Shangri-La, but that's fiction. In fact, the rich, successful daddy may be one of the most ineffectual. *Ladies' Home Journal* and Gallup did a survey a few years ago with some revealing results. They showed that "college-educated and economically better-off fathers, although they can provide their daughters with material and intellectual advantages, spend the least amount of time with them, do the least things for them, and seem the least outwardly loving."

On the other hand, a woman who compared her husband to her father said, "My father never went to college and he worked hard to earn a living, but he made time for me and my sister. My husband has it a lot easier, but he spends almost all his free time at sports, especially tennis. If he could just turn our daughter into an athlete, he'd be glad to spend time with her."

Next, the survey showed that the father who was most satisfied with the job he did as a parent is likely to have had a good marriage, and vice versa.[20]

Good fathers teach their daughters sportsmanship, courage, and respect for hard work. One young father said that his teenage daughter looked to him for guidance, goals, and lifestyle, and to her mother for personal advice and sharing romantic and emotional matters.

It is a fearsome thing to be describing the traits of a good father, as I stand before the four Jeremiah offspring in all my vulnerability. First, it may lead my children to suppose that I can replace God, and that I cannot do. While fathers blunder, God stands firm; while we make mistakes, He is infallible; while we may seem to place restrictions on our love, He loves unconditionally. Next, in believing he is a good father, a man may sound as if he has the guaranteed seal of approval for success in raising his children. Author and professor Thomas Howard said, "I will write no books or articles on successful fatherhood—at least not until I am ninety and both my children have turned out to be aging saints, and have raised their own crops of mature saints. Any time before that is too soon."[21]

I know that the place for fathers to be while raising their daughters (and sons, too) is on their knees. When I think of what I want most for my girls, I pray that God will protect them through the vulnerable years. There is such a fine line between falling off that tightrope of the teens and walking across safely to the beginning of maturity. I want to be the kind of dad who not only provides the steadying hand, but also holds the life-saving net.

BUT IT'S NEVER TOO LATE

Maybe, dads, as you've read this chapter you've agreed with the principles, but your daughter is now grown up. There's always hope, and it's never too late to start developing a better relationship.

Charlie Shedd tells about a dad who knocked on his daughter's door one night soon after she'd gone to bed. When she told him to come in, he sat down and made a little speech something like this:

"Vicky, I want to apologize. I want you to know I'm sorry for a silly thing I've done. You're a senior in high school now, and all these years I've been saying that someday I'd take time for us to get acquainted. So, here you are with nine months left at our house, then you'll be going away to college and getting married, and Lord only knows how far we'll be from each other. So, I want to ask you to do me a favor. Once every week in this senior year, I'd like to take you out alone for a meal so we can have time to talk together. I know you're busy evenings, and I can't get away for lunch. But, maybe we can get up early and go out for breakfast, just the two of us. That's the invitation. Take some time to think it over and let me know how you feel."[22]

There's a song by Steve and Annie Chapman which says it well:

> Daddy, you're the man in your little girl's dreams,
> You are the one she longs to please.
> And there's a place in her heart
> That can only be filled by her daddy's love.
> But if you don't give her the love she desires,
> She'll try someone else, but they won't satisfy her.
> And if your little girl grows up
> Without Daddy's love,
> She may feel empty, and it's only because
> It's her daddy's love that she's looking for.
> Don't send her away to another man's door.
> Nobody else can do what you do.
> She just needs her daddy's love.[23]

Have you given your little girl her daddy's love? If you haven't, tell her you love her and that she is the most precious girl in the world to you. It's never too late.

The time is now to repair any weak threads in a father-daughter relationship. Solomon said, "If you wait for perfect conditions, you will never get anything done" (Ecclesiastes 11:4, TLB).

So, Dad, make a date now with a very important woman in your life, your daughter.

MYTH FOUR

He's Daddy's Boy

*O*ne of our church members slipped me a cartoon which showed two little boys walking to school and discussing the problems of growing up with parents. One boy said to his friend, "I figured out a system for getting along with my mom. She tells me what to do and I do it."

Moms may have the bulk of the child-rearing responsibilities when the children are small, but when a boy reaches a certain age, It's usually assumed that Dad is the most influential and Mom should retreat to the background. After all, it is reasoned, "Dads are for sons," and we don't want to have sissy Mama's boys. The fallacy here is that the influence of a mother is less important than that of a dad—and that mothers and sons do not form as strong a bond.

There is an old Spanish proverb that says, "An ounce of mother is worth a pound of clergy." I believe that proverb, for I have lived long enough to see it proven. There have been many men who have deeply influenced my life, but not one of them has taught me half as much as I learned from the life of my mother. Though I obviously believe in the ministry of the clergy, the ministry of godly men can never undo the lack of ministry by the mothers of our day. When God wanted to send His Son into this world, He chose a woman through whom He would work His miracle.

History tells of many mothers who have influenced the world through their sons. St. Augustine might never have become the great church leader he was, had it not been for the prayers of Monica, his mother; Rembrandt, the famous Dutch artist, may never have given us his beautiful biblical paintings had he not been inspired by his mother.

In the history of outstanding Christian leaders, the story of Hudson Taylor is legend. He was a great missionary to China, the

63

founder of the China Inland Mission, which was the first truly interdenominational foreign mission and the prototype of the "faith" missions that played a prominent part in world evangelization in the nineteenth century. Years before his missionary work began, Taylor's mother intensely desired to know that her son was converted. One day while she was miles away from her son, she excused herself from a meeting to get alone and pray for his salvation. It was during her prayer time that he became a believer in Jesus Christ.

Jonathan Edwards, the famous revivalist and brilliant preacher, was converted early in life through the witness of a Christian mother. Likewise, John and Charles Wesley, founders of Methodism, were two of nineteen children whom their mother prayed into the Kingdom of God.

Billy Graham wrote a tribute to his mother in his book, *Facing Death and the Life After:* "She was one of the most beautiful women I have ever known, and she instilled in me a love for the Bible, even when it didn't seem to interest me. She began to read to my brother and sisters from devotionals and many times I thought them extremely boring . . . Although the testimony of my mother's life helped mold me and taught me how to live, the testimony of her last years and her death gave me insight into how to die."[1]

If you ever watch college football, when the camera pans the faces of the players, some of them will inevitably grin and wave, "Hi, Mom."

I read a survey that asked boys who they would be most likely to confide in if they had a problem, and about 23 percent said their father. The remaining 77 percent said they would confide in their mother.

One of my observations about my son David, who is seventeen and in his junior year in high school at the time of this writing, is that most of the in-depth conversations he has with his parents take place with Donna. And I have just begun to realize that what I learn about the important things in David's life come through my wife, rather than from him directly. I've seen him with Donna, sitting on his bed, or at the kitchen table, engrossed in conversation; when he wants permission to use the car or have a special date, he talks to her about it, and then she talks to me. I don't mind that, but it clearly illustrates the closeness a teenage boy feels with his mother.

I think the contribution a mother makes to her son's life is similar to the father-daughter influence. A mother helps her son formulate the kind of woman he wants for a wife; she encourages a boy to develop the softer side of his nature and teaches him that he is unconditionally accepted.

WHERE CAN YOU FIND A MODEL MOTHER?

From the very beginning, God has given us examples of the sorrows and joys of mothers and sons. Eve's first, most beloved, son killed his brother. What anguish the original mother must have felt as a result of that tragic happening. She experienced all the heartaches that mothers of wicked sons throughout the ages have suffered, and yet Eve knew that God was still in charge of the universe which He had created. Many years after Cain murdered Abel, Eve gave birth to a son whom she named Seth, meaning "to appoint" or "to establish." And what a son he was! The ancestry of Jesus Christ was to be traced back to the line of Seth.

Another outstanding model of motherhood from the Old Testament is Hannah. Her name means "gracious" or "favor," and for the past three thousand years, millions of little Anns, Annes, or Annas have had names that reflect the influence of this great woman; however, it is from her relationship to her son that we may find the most inspiring source of imitation.

The social environment of Hannah's time was not the best, any more than our times are a model of morality. The people of Israel had fallen from the high standards set by Moses. Hannah's own life was blighted because she had no children. It was the burning desire of every Hebrew parent to have a son, and she was barren. But Hannah believed with all of her heart that God was the Creator of children and at His will He could make a woman a mother.

For years Hannah prayed for a son and withstood the taunts of her husband's other wife, Peninnah, who had sons and daughters. In those polygamous times it must have been very difficult for Hannah, who was her husband's favorite wife, to maintain an attitude of prayer and submission while living in the same household with the jealous Peninnah and listening to her cruel words. To make matters worse, one day Hannah was in the temple praying inaudibly, with just her lips moving, when Eli, the priest, accused her of being drunk. (Is there anything harder for us to handle than unjustified criticism?) However, Hannah's integrity showed in her defense when she answered the priest, "Not so, my lord . . . I am a woman who is deeply troubled. I have not been drinking wine or beer; I was pouring out my soul to the Lord. Do not take your servant for a wicked woman; I have been praying here out of my great anguish and grief" (1 Samuel 1:15–16).

Firm in her belief that God would answer her prayer for a son, Hannah was willing to pray again and again. She even promised to give the child back to God "for all the days of his life." When her fervent prayer was finally answered and she had her long-awaited baby boy, she named him Samuel, which means "asked of the Lord."

She nursed and took care of little Samuel, giving him all the love a devoted mother has for her first baby. However, when Samuel was weaned, she dressed him in his best clothes and took him to the tabernacle where she left him with Eli, telling the priest that she had prayed for this child and now she would give her little boy back to the Lord as she had promised. Eli had not done such a good job in raising his own sons, but Hannah was confident that the Lord would care for Samuel. She said a prayer of thanksgiving, even though her mother's heart must have been aching at the thought of not being able to see her son more than once a year, when she would come with her husband to offer the annual sacrifice. The boy, Samuel, became the earliest of the great Hebrew prophets after Moses and the last of the judges of Israel.

The last part of Hannah's story tells us that "the boy Samuel grew up in the presence of the Lord" (1 Samuel 2:21). This bears a fascinating similarity to the story of Jesus who went to the temple at Jerusalem, and He, too, "grew in wisdom and stature, and in favor with God and men" (Luke 2:52).

Hannah, like Mary, gave her son to God and then slipped into the background, becoming a vital part of human history through her son. Hannah was a prayerful mother who was willing to turn the outcome of her son's life over to the Lord.

BLESSED AMONG WOMEN

If you were to ask most literate people, "Who was the most important mother in history?" whether they were believers or unbelievers, they would undoubtedly say, "Mary, the mother of Jesus."

She has been the subject of more art, music, and literature than any other woman. No woman has had more baby girls named after her; more poems, carols, or lullabies written about her; more portraits painted of her than the woman whom her cousin Elizabeth proclaimed: "Blessed . . . among women" (Luke 1:42).

> Though Mary herself never wore fine clothes, the Madonnas through the ages have been draped in the most costly of garments, and people have left at her feet the world's most precious jewels. Though she never exalted herself, literature has raised her to the highest pinnacle of any woman in history. Though she never entered a palace, her picture has graced the most magnificent palaces. Though she never traveled any farther than from Palestine to Egypt, and then by donkey, her story still travels to the farthest corners of the earth. And though she suffered as much as any woman in the world's history, her suffering changed to joy at her son's resurrection.[2]

The story of Mary and the birth of Jesus has probably been heard more than any other story in Scripture, and yet there are millions of people on earth who don't believe it, or if they do believe, they are unable to grasp its meaning in their own lives. Mary was chosen by God to bring the Savior into the world. Her hymn of praise to God is one of the most jubilant songs ever recorded (Luke 1:46–55), and an indication that she knew the Psalms and the song of Hannah. The Magnificat is a praise prayer to which mothers of the world can turn for new faith and belief in the Creator.

It is difficult, if not impossible, for most mothers to relate to Mary. However, it is her attitude, not her circumstances, that is the model for women today. No mother's pain could be greater than the pain Mary experienced at the Cross. She stood and witnessed the degradation of her Son, watching His suffering for hours—not sitting, as others might, but standing by the cross.

> As He dies, she stands in silence. Those around her had no conception of her inner grief as she stood where her Son could see her. No Spartan mother ever displayed such fortitude as Mary manifested at the Cross. How impressed we are with the valor of Mary, as the sword pierces her heart again "now that He which she brought forth was dying"! . . . Some of His disciples forsook Him and fled, but her love never surrendered, even though her Son was dying as a criminal between two thieves.[3]

Mary's silent endurance of what she could not change is the great lesson she exemplified at the Cross. Although Mary has been exalted and elevated to a position which the Scriptures do not contain, she is the world's most beautiful example of motherhood.

How can Mary be a model to all the mothers who are saying, "There is no connection between Mary and my relationship with my son . . . it's almost sacrilegious to think of such a thing!" And yet Mary had conflicts which are common to other mothers. For one thing, she must have had a sense of participating in a drama she couldn't comprehend. How many mothers look at their children and wonder, *what's going to happen to them in this crazy world?* No doubt, she also experienced the mental vacillation between asserting parental authority and allowing the child increasing freedom. Those conflicts are common to all mothers. Mary prayed, praised, and trusted. These are the qualities all mothers (and fathers, too) would do well to model.

WHERE'S MOM TODAY?

He runs in from school, checks the refrigerator, and then looks for the inevitable note. "Dear Tommy: Don't eat more than three cookies. Jello in the refrig is for supper. Do your homework before any TV. If anyone calls say I'll be back in a minute and get the name. I have to work until seven o'clock, so feed the dog, and if Dad gets home before I do, ask him to start the spaghetti. Love, Mom."

Today's mother is more likely to be in the office, the store, or the factory, than home when Tommy gets out of school. She may be raising the kids alone or adding to the family income, but, for whatever reasons, millions of U.S. families face what *Time* magazine called "a wrenching question: Who's minding the kids?" Our generation has coined the term "latchkey kids." With child-care centers for their chief source of direction, or television for a teacher and babysitter, a generation of kids is being raised who don't even know what parents are for. The trend is not encouraging; fifteen years ago a third of all American families could be considered "traditional," that is, mother at home and father the sole support. But today, less than a fifth of U.S. families would fall into that category. "Today more than 60 percent of mothers with children under 14 are in the labor force."[4]

Anxiety about the care of their children is gnawing at responsible moms and dads. Reliable day-care centers are hard to find. Relatives have scattered, and Grandma wants to live her own life. Kids are getting mixed signals because discipline and order are not consistent. "'It is scaring everybody that a whole generation of children is being raised in a way that has never happened before,' says Edward Zigler, professor of psychology at Yale and an authority on child care."[5]

The problem is so pervasive that one working mother remarked, "Finding someone to help raise your child is the hardest thing you'll ever have to do."

Why has this happened in what we might call the Snowball Syndrome? It began to roll in the '60s with the outset of the feminist movement, which encouraged housewives to become more "fulfilled" by pursuing a career, and picked up speed in the '70s and '80s as inflation eroded the middle-class goals of a house, a car, and an education for the kids. Almost overnight it seemed that the Great American Dream had a dual-income price tag. These two trends, multiplied by the material "more and more" philosophy, have seen Mom trade in her apron for a briefcase.

For many women, the legacy of being raised in the 1950s, at a time when her mother was home making apple pies and having dinner ready when Dad came in from the office, has been denied by the facts of the 1980s. One woman said, "Thirty years ago, our mothers enjoyed the camaraderie of women with shared goals. The large majority of women stayed home. Today only seven percent of households fall into the traditional category—a working father, a housewife and one or more children at home. The homogeneity that gave our mothers comfort does not exist for us. Today our lives are fractured and we are insecure, cautious of one another, defensive about the roles we've assumed."[6]

As I heard someone say not long ago, "It used to be when a boy couldn't learn at his mother's knee, he found himself over his father's." Perhaps today that boy would be found sitting in front of the TV like a zombie, watching the same cartoons or game shows over and over again.

A few years ago I ran across an article called "Money, Memories, and Motherhood," which was written after one woman became concerned about the importance of fulfilling the God-given role of a woman. She said:

> Recently an economist estimated the amount of money that a mother could earn if she worked rather than staying home with her

children for their first 14 years. So I decided to do a little figuring of my own.

I soon discovered that if I had worked full time through these past 14 years (we have children on both sides of age 14), I could have earned about $65,000 more than I have earned by working just part time for a few of those years. Immediately, I envisioned the larger home (paid for), the bigger car, a healthy savings account, vacations or perhaps a swimming pool. So, logically, I asked myself why I had elected to pass up such a bounty.

The answer wasn't long in coming. It was a kaleidoscope of events, small vacations, that occurred through the years. I thought about a small red-haired boy, playing outside as I watched from the kitchen window, wearing his brother's football helmet, riding his tricycle, and pretending he was a traffic policeman.

Still thinking of the $65,000, I asked, "If I could turn time back 14 years, would I make the same decision?" The answer is, "Yes." If I have learned one thing about life, it is that happiness doesn't result from bigger houses and bigger cars. Happiness is derived mainly from our association with people whom we care about.

The wealth I have accumulated is not in possessions but in moments, past and present, that have allowed me to share for a few years in the lives of these children. These moments are worth a million dollars to me. According to my calculations, that makes me $935,000 richer than I would have been if I had not been there when they were growing up.[7]

She said it well. A working mother in a dual-income family has hard choices to make. She knows she may be exchanging a child's security for a new car, a few years of extra buying for a lifetime of memories. An increasing number of mothers with young children are seeking part-time work and delaying a full-time career until later. It's been said that the hand that rocks the cradle rules the world. Can we speculate what will be the outcome for America when that hand is working the typewriter, running the computers, or managing the businesses?

HOW CAN MOTHERS RAISE BOLD LEADERS?

In today's climate, with AIDS in the epidemic stage and homosexuality more prevalent than at any time in history, there is more need than ever for mothers to understand their role in their sons' lives. Dominant mothers can foster weak sons who turn to their own sex for solace and love. On the other hand, leadership is learned by sons from their fathers, but is encouraged by the example of a wife who can show a submissive, loving spirit toward her husband. The worst thing a mother does to abort a son's leadership is to take over the role of leader in the family.

My father demanded that we show respect to our mother, and I have followed his example. One of the things I've done with David, for instance, is to take him shopping for a gift for Donna at special times. I want him to know how important she is to me, so that he will have a greater understanding of our relationship. This all ties in to mothers and sons, for without the man being the head of the family, sons will grow up with a distorted view of the roles of women.

BIBLICAL PRINCIPLES OF SUCCESS

If we examine the lives of a couple of outstanding Old Testament mothers—Miriam, mother of Moses, and Hannah, mother of Samuel—we find six principles of success for raising boys that are not found in *Ladies' Home Journal* or *Family Living*. By using these same principles, mothers today may find little need for the "How to" articles which are currently so popular.

Principle One: *Be a mother of faith.* "By faith Moses' parents hid him for three months after he was born, because they saw he was no ordinary child, and they were not afraid of the king's edict" (Hebrews 11:23).

It's difficult to imagine that Moses' mother put him in a little basket and set him down among the crocodiles. However, putting your child's life in the care of health professionals may be just as frightening as seeing your baby drifting down the Nile. Every mother who has had the terrifying experience of a child's sudden illness knows the difficulty of trusting the Lord for his safety.

We have been entrusted with these lives for a time and only God can give inexperienced human beings the wisdom to train exuberant, bouncing, accident-prone, wild little creatures into mature manhood.

Principle Two: *Be careful not to be overprotective.* Moses' mother and Samuel's mother put their sons in God's hands with prayers in their hearts. A boy may be robbed of his self-esteem and confidence by a mother who is constantly saying, "Be careful, now . . . watch out . . . don't get hurt." One man told me that his mother had programmed him as a youngster to believe he was a "delicate child." As he grew up, he avoided sports because she was afraid he would catch cold or be hurt. He struggled with his concept of manhood and compensated by overdrinking. A boy needs to explore, rough-house, get dirty, and try new things without a worried mother hovering over him.

> A boy may be robbed of his self-esteem and confidence by a mother who is constantly saying, "Be careful, now . . . watch out . . . don't get hurt."

Most mothers have a certain protective instinct built into their make-up. I have seen Donna drive her fingernails into the palms of her hands when one of our kids was tackled during a football game or knocked to the ground on the basketball court. One year her concern for David, the quarterback for our Christian High School team, made the sports page of our local newspaper. The headline read, "Stakes are high for protecting Patriot."

Donna had a brilliant idea to motivate the team members and protect her oldest son (and her own nervous system) from physical and mental stress. For every game in which David was not sacked, she would treat his offensive linemen to a steak dinner. In the next game our team had a 21–0 victory and the offensive line did a great job. "Steak dinners for no sacks," David told the men. However, he added, "It was my mom's idea . . . kind of a safety precaution." So far Donna has prepared a lot of steak dinners.

Principle Three: *Teach your children at home.* Too often parents believe that if their children are in Sunday school every week, if they have learned the memory verses which are required to earn their gold stars on the chart, and if they pray before meals, then that is sufficient for their spiritual growth.

Remember how Samuel was sent to Eli, the priest? Eli, of course, had some no-good sons, and Samuel must have grown up with those fellows; however, as a result of his mother's early teaching, and her continual prayers, Samuel grew up to be a great man of God.

Timothy was the young man of whom the apostle Paul said, "I

have been reminded of your sincere faith, which first lived in your grandmother Lois and in your mother Eunice, and, I am persuaded, now lives in you also" (2 Timothy 1:5).

Today there are Bible stories to read, cassettes to hear, and games to play. Never before has there been such an abundance of Christian music and concerts. Learn some of the catchy songs that children enjoy; sing them when you're in the car or around the house. Too many kids seem to know more jingles from television commercials than they do songs about Jesus.

Principle Four: *Teach them that they're special.* As kids grow up they have many forces attempting to discourage their potential; they need all the reinforcement we can give them. I cringe when I hear a parent say in his or her child's presence, "He's really very bashful," or speak some other trait into existence by emphasizing it. Calling a son "Stupid," "Knucklehead," "Dummy," "Stumblebum," or some other name, even in fun, makes an impression on him which he will unconsciously follow.

We can see how important self esteem is from this true story. A certain boy's mother was a dominating person, who displayed no love for anyone. She had been married three times, and her second husband divorced her because she abused him. The child never experienced love or discipline; he was just shoved around.

His mother told him, "Don't ever bother me at work; I don't want you pestering me." He was totally rejected. He had a high I.Q., but dropped out of high school. He joined the Marines, but was given a dishonorable discharge. He had no talent or skill; he didn't even have a driver's license.

He traveled to a foreign country, met a woman and soon their marriage began to fail. His wife rejected him, but he begged her to let him come back. Soon afterward he returned to the United States. The only talent he had was handling a rifle, and on November 22, 1963, he used this ability from the third story of a book storage building in Dallas, Texas, to fire three shots that changed the course of a nation. His name was Lee Harvey Oswald.[8]

His home life, from childhood to adulthood, neglected to give him three important factors: love, discipline, and a sense of self-worth.

Of course, Oswald is an extreme example of what can happen to children who are rejected, but sometimes we need an impression painted in vivid, living color to jolt us to reinforce the special qualities our sons possess.

Principle Five: *Teach your son responsibility.* One mother said she told her boy, "I don't care what job, business, or profession you choose, but one thing that will carry you far in whatever you choose is to develop a sense of *responsibility.*"

I shall never forget my own mother in this regard. One of the things she insisted I do was to make my bed and clean my room before I went to school. I did everything I could to avoid that responsibility; I would get my lunch ready, my books under my arm, and try to sneak out of the house. When I got home at night, I would get a scolding. She said, "If you don't start being responsible, I'll do everything I can to make the lesson clear to you." One day, when I was in eighth grade, she made that threat a reality. I was innocently working on a report in study hall when the principal called me into his office. He said, "Your mother is here to take you home. She said you didn't make your bed and straighten your room before school, and that is your responsibility. I thoroughly agree with her, and therefore you will be marked absent for this period and you may not return to school until you have fulfilled your obligations."

It wasn't long before the word spread around school that Jeremiah had to go home to make his bed. Believe me, that lesson left a lasting impression on me.

Most boys are not responsible by nature, but by training. Make a list, post deadlines for tasks to be done, and avoid the nagging. If a job is unsatisfactory, have him repeat it. "Isn't there something you forgot?" is much kinder than saying with an exasperated sigh, "Can't you ever do anything right the first time?" We learn by making mistakes.

> **Most boys are not responsible by nature, but by training.**

Keeping a sense of humor is essential in teaching our children and keeping our sanity. One mother told me that after pleading, demanding, and cajoling her son to pick up his clothes, she draped them on the lamppost outside the front door and when he came home from school they were waving merrily in the breeze. She simply said, "That's where all of your clothes will be that you leave on the floor." The boy has grown into a young man and still tells the story on himself.

Principle Six: *Show sons that their father has the final authority.* By doing this, a mother teaches her sons to be strong leaders for God, secure in their masculinity. After all, a boy is the only thing God can use to make a man.

Motto for mothers:

> Give of thy sons to bear the message glorious.
> Give of thy wealth to speed them on their way.
> Pour out your souls for them in prayer victorious,
> And all thou spendest Jesus will repay.[9]

MYTH FIVE

A Chapter a Day
Keeps the Devil Away

A woman had two incorrigible little boys who were driving her to the edge of despair. She had exhausted all the disciplinary methods she knew. To no avail, she had suffered the criticism and advice of family and friends. She even took her boys to a child psychologist, whose recommendations were useless; she joined a special class in understanding children, but no matter what she tried, they only seemed to get worse.

One day she was talking to a fine Christian woman who put her arm around the distraught mother and said, "I know what you're going through. I had a son similar to your children, and I took him to see my pastor. I don't know what he said to him, but I do know that from the moment he came out of his office, he was a changed person."

The mother said, "But I don't go to your church. Would your pastor see my boys?" The woman assured her he would.

She took the advice of her friend and made an appointment with the minister, dragging her objecting sons all the way. After introducing her older boy, she told the younger one to stay in the waiting room, and she went outside to sit in the car until they were finished. She did not want to face the embarrassment of seeing the pastor after what she knew would be a futile encounter with her boys.

The older boy was frightened; he had never been one-on-one with a pastor in his life, and he wasn't sure what authority he had. The minister, a tall, imposing man with laugh lines around his eyes, was silent for a while, scrutinizing the sulky face of the boy in front of him. After what seemed an eternity to the child, he said, "Young man, where is God?" The boy had no idea what he was expected to say, so he sat in silence. The minister repeated the question, this time with a more commanding tone in his voice. "Young man, where

79

is God?" The boy looked around at the artifacts in the office, as if the answer might be found there. Finally, becoming more insistent, the pastor thundered, "Young man, I said, 'Where is God?'"

The boy jumped out of the chair, ran from the room, grabbed his little brother and raced out of the waiting room. He shouted, "Johnny, they've lost God and they're trying to pin it on us."

The story may be fiction, but the truth is that is what has happened in many homes. God is still there, but He is lost. We dare not allow that to happen in Christian families.

Many Christian parents believe if they could just sit down with their children for a scheduled time each day and have devotions, they would have the magic potion to immunize their family against the disease of secular humanism that has spread its plague in our national life. But they are frustrated because they don't have time, or their children's ages are too different for the same story, or they don't want to force the kids to endure a boring lesson. The excuses seem valid, but the answers to the dilemma are not always apparent. Take heart, Christian parents. This idea that daily family devotions or "a chapter a day" is a cure-all for spiritual malaise is a myth.

STAMPING ON SACRED GROUND

Donna and I come from strong Christian backgrounds where devotions were regularly read after supper. Sometimes these exercises in daily lessons were meaningless to us and caused frustrations in our lives. I remember one time my father thought we should read through *Pilgrim's Progress;* I don't know whether it was my age or my lack of literary interest at that time, but I was so bored. Years later I appreciated that wonderful classic, but not as a restless boy.

After Donna and I were married we decided that our family would not be that structured. When Jan and David were five or six years old my parents said they wanted to take them on a camping trip. Since that was never my favorite form of recreation, we were delighted to send the kids off with Grandma and Grandpa. The first evening at the campsite, the four of them finished dinner and my father said, "Come on, kids, it's time for devotions." Brother and sister looked at each other and almost in unison said, "What's devotions?"

When they returned from that little vacation my dad must have been concerned about the kind of family we were raising, but he didn't say anything until later.

As I look back on my boyhood, it hasn't been the planned "devotional times" that have remained in my memory. In fact, I recall those times having very little meaning for me. However, it was seeing Mother come out of her room with tears on her cheeks after communing intimately with God, or observing Dad's attitude of kindness, patience, fairness, and love as he weathered the storms of pressure and criticism in his job as president of a growing Christian college, that have impressed my life. I watched Mother give of herself and her time to help people in need. The lasting values for my life were not in daily devotions, but in recognizing love in action and glimpsing the flow of God's Spirit in the everyday routine of living.

Some unknown poet wrote:

> I saw you stand bravely through the years
> And saw no sign of senseless fears
> I saw you stand quietly through the stress
> And saw no glimpse of bitterness
> I saw you stand prayerfully in grief
> And saw no sign of unbelief
> Though you spoke well of Jesus Christ
> I caught your faith by watching your life.

A study was made of one thousand Presbyterian families, and it was determined that seven out of ten families had grace at meals, but only one in twenty had Scripture reading in family groups.[1] If a survey such as this is representative of contemporary Protestants, we must conclude that traditional "family devotions" are not being used to meet the needs of church families today. What, then, is the answer?

I do not discount the value of a family altar or other specific times of learning about God in the home, but I am concerned about parents who never miss family devotions, but live weak and emaciated Christian lives. They remind me of the following words: "Whatever parent gives his children good instruction and sets for them at the same time a bad example, may be considered as bringing them food in one hand and poison in the other."

Christian psychologists Paul and Richard Meier tell this true story:

Jack M. was a forty-five-year-old father who was being treated in our psychiatry ward for alcoholism. During a group therapy session, Mr. M. avoided discussing his own problems by bragging to the group about what a good disciplinarian he was with his children. He told us that he made his children go to church every Sunday morning, Sunday night, and Wednesday night. When a group member asked him if he went with them, he replied, "Well, no, I don't, because I'm too restless and can't sit still that long." Then he bragged about how he made his children study their school work for one hour every night and also read their Bible every night. I asked him if he studied very much or read his Bible every day. He replied, "Well, no, I don't, because I get bored too easy when I read." Mr. M. still went on to brag that he didn't let his children watch any television whatsoever. When a group member asked him why, he replied, "Because there's too many beer commercials on TV." I asked him what he had been doing every night for the past few years, and he finally admitted, "I've been sitting at home watching television every night and drinking about a fifth of whiskey."

He was offended that we made him aware of the fact that he was setting a poor example for his children. His children will probably turn out the very opposite of what he wants, because he is telling them one thing and practicing another.[2]

GOD'S DIRECTIONS FOR FAMILY DEVOTIONS

"These commandments that I give you today are to be upon your hearts. Impress them on your children. Talk about them when you sit at home and when you walk along the road, when you lie down and when you get up. Tie them as symbols on your hands and bind them on your foreheads. Write them on the doorframes of your houses and on your gates" (Deuteronomy 6:6–9).

PRACTICAL LESSONS FROM JEWISH TRADITION

The devout Jewish parent of today has traditions for the religious training of his children that have applications to Christian parents. For example, in a special synagogue service, a Jewish child kisses a drop of honey that has been placed on a copy of the Torah. In this way, the youngster tastes the Word which is "sweeter than honey, than honey from the comb" (Psalms 19:10). If we develop in our children a hunger to taste God's Word and feed upon it regularly, we are obeying the first part of the command God gave to Moses to have the Word "upon your heart."

Dennis Fisher wrote: "Not long ago Sarah, my seven-year-old daughter, and I tasted the 'sweetness' of the Word together. She had shown considerable interest in reading at school and I asked if she would be interested in reading directly from the Bible to me on a regular basis. We would use her own Bible and examine a paragraph at a time. She became excited by the idea, ran into her bedroom to get her Bible and what began as a father-daughter experiment in Bible reading has now become a family custom. We look forward to our reading, and I have often experienced a sense of God's presence and felt the Holy Spirit illuminate the passage as Sarah reads it. It 'tastes good.'"[3]

This idea of "impressing" (see Deuteronomy 6:7) the words on children or teaching them is taken from the Hebrew word which meant to sharpen a sword for battle. Raising a child requires constant attention, just as a much used sword needs careful honing. Formal training can never take the place of family living.

> Formal training can never take the place of family living.

Moses told the Jews to "tie" God's commands as "symbols on your hands and bind them on your foreheads." Some Orthodox Jews take this verse so literally that they attach two boxes containing passages from the Bible to the left arm and the upper part of the forehead during morning prayer; these are called phylacteries. This practice serves as a reminder that God's Word should dwell within their hearts and be the focus of their thoughts and deeds throughout the day.

Another spiritual reminder of God's command in Jewish tradition is the "mezuzah," which is a little wooden or metal box you'll find at the door of Jewish homes and synagogues. It contains a piece of parchment on which is written some verses from Deuteronomy and

Shaddai, one of the Hebrew names for God. The word *Shaddai* shows through an opening in the mezuzah, reminding people of God's presence.

In the musical *Fiddler on the Roof,* Tevye sang that memorable song about "tradition." God has used family traditions to preserve the Jews throughout the ages; one of the most important of these customs is Passover. As a part of this traditional ceremony, the youngest child asks, "Father, why is this night different from any other?" The father explains the significance of the first Passover when the Jews were delivered from Egyptian bondage by the Lord; everyone in the family listens to the youngest child with respect. Can you imagine the impression that would make on a youngster?

Kids, however, do not always get the right impressions from church rituals. Trisha was very attentive as she witnessed her first baptismal service. The next day her mother was walking down the hall when she heard Trisha's voice coming from the bathroom. When she got to the door, she looked in and saw her little girl with all of her dolls leaning against the bathtub, and she was baptising them one by one. She was repeating the words of the pastor she had heard the night before . . . at least what she thought she had heard.

Each time she immersed a doll, Trisha said very solemnly, "In the name of the Father, and the Son, and in the hole you go."

PRACTICAL LESSONS FOR CHRISTIANS

When Moses said that God's Word must be "upon your hearts" (Deuteronomy 6:6), he meant that it is to be a burden, something that grips us. This passage in Deuteronomy has so much for us living in America today. We cannot impart what we do not possess. It is senseless to pray, "Lord, make my children more patient," if we have no patience ourselves. It's hypocritical to drop off the children at church or leave their spiritual growth to the one-hour-a-week teaching of an overworked volunteer. When we do this, they learn an important lesson: "Do as I say, not as I do"—not exactly the lesson we had in mind. Just as we need the leadership of our heavenly Leader, our children need the leadership of their parents.

One year our family spent two weeks of vacation in Ocean City,

New Jersey. We lived in a beach house and spent many hours walking along the beautiful white sandy shore. After supper one evening, we decided to stroll along the beach to the boardwalk, about twenty blocks away. It was 7:00 P.M. when we started out toward the city; low tide was to be at 7:30.

As we approached the lights of the crowded boardwalk, the ocean was emptying itself of all its contents and depositing them on the sand; the ugly and the beautiful were all around us. I remember pointing out to the children that they ought to be careful where they walked. We were barefoot and could easily step on broken shells or those horrid jellyfish.

When we reached our destination and decided to return to our beach house, the shoreline was covered with all of the debris the ocean has regurgitated. Since my gait is usually about twice as fast as anyone else's, I was walking out in front of the rest of the family. Suddenly I sensed that someone was immediately behind me. I could almost feel his breath. The crunch of feet, not my own, was audible and I looked over my shoulder to see one small son stretching to put his feet in the very footprints I was leaving in the sand. I guess he felt that the only way he could be sure that he avoided broken shells, jellyfish, and crabs was to step exactly where his father was stepping.

What a lesson I learned that day! Sometimes as I walk through the debris of this world, I shudder to think of all the spiritual jellyfish, broken shells, and crabs that lie in the path. There is no certain way to avoid these pitfalls apart from the steps of our heavenly Leader.

Christian education is a daily experience of Christ. It is loving Him, knowing Him, and following Him. A parent must know, show, and go the way.

"Talk about them when you sit at home and when you walk along the road, when you lie down and when you get up" (Deuteronomy 6:7). This type of teaching is a full-time occupation. Most substitutes cannot replace the value of a parent's instruction.

A NIGHT TO REMEMBER

One time I decided to take my two oldest children camping. I didn't know very much about the skills of this endeavor, just that it's supposed to be a good experience for kids and that my two were excited about it. We were scheduled to leave about 5:00 P.M., but some emergency came up and I couldn't get away, so it was 9:30 by the time I was ready. We were going to Pokagon Camp (the kids probably thought it should be called Poke-Along because of the way their dad was acting). We had a borrowed tent which I had never put up before, and before we left I had rehearsed my hopeful question: "You kids don't really want to go tonight, do you?" Was I kidding? They were so ready to go they were waiting in the driveway.

I had promised them the trip, so we went. We reached the camp after dark and had one little lantern to guide us while we set up our tent; in the process of getting out of the car one of the kids dropped the lantern and it broke! We struggled with the canvas and ropes in the pitch blackness of Pokagon and somehow figured it out and got the thing up. We crawled in the best we could and went to sleep.

When I woke up the next morning, we were all in a little ball down at the bottom of the tent. We had set the tent up on a slope and through the night we had slid right to the bottom and there we were, like three bears huddled in a canvas cave. Outside our cocoon we heard a strange rattling of cans and crunching of leaves. We climbed through the flap and watched a family of raccoons scurrying away from our campsite. That morning we went horseback riding and talked about the wonder of God's creation, the fascinating variety of animals, and the beauty surrounding us in the woods.

When my children talk about the things they remember, it is the night out at Pokagon that is always mentioned. Something about that experience brought us together; it was a rich and exciting time talking about God's creation. Maybe I taught more that night than I had taught in the last two years seated around the dinner table.

JESUS, OUR MODEL

In His humanity, Jesus is the standard, the ideal, for our modeling, even in our roles as parents. But His words could not have an impact on our lives if they didn't match His actions. In studying the life of Jesus, I have found six ways He shows us how to be better parents by matching our words with our actions.

First, *Jesus was open and spontaneous.* He was not tied to strict traditions, nor was He concerned about impressing others. He talked with a Samaritan woman at a well, an act which surprised (and, perhaps, shocked) His disciples. He washed the feet of His disciples, even though He was their Master.

When we are spontaneous with our children we may have many unplanned adventures together: slowing the car to look at a rainbow, having a surprise party for no reason, stopping what we're doing to examine a treasure. Spontaneity is capturing magic moments at unexpected times.

Jesus accepted people; He was without prejudice. He was a friend of both Jews and Gentiles. He was at ease with the poor and the wealthy. He surrounded himself with people from all backgrounds: detested tax collectors, working men, lepers, the educated and the uneducated. He did not have the attitude of being better than anyone.

Our children observe and imitate our prejudices. If we tell malicious jokes about other races or ethnic groups, we are giving messages of prejudice. If we treat people according to the size of their bank accounts, we send out strong signals of discrimination, which our children will tune in on.

Jesus had a sense of humor. His parables contained amusing illustrations, such as a camel going through the eye of a needle, or tax collectors getting into heaven ahead of priests. He enjoyed being in the company of people so much that His enemies accused Him of being a drunkard and a glutton.

We do not have to be stand-up comedians to exhibit humor. For some of us, jokes and funny stories do not come naturally. However, we can all learn not to take ourselves too seriously, to laugh more and frown less. In Proverbs we're reminded: "A happy heart makes the face cheerful" (Proverbs 15:31). The most admired people we know are the ones who are fun to be around.

Jesus taught that it is good to spend time alone. He left the multitude to pray and meditate. He needed privacy when pressures were intense. He showed the need to leave the crowd and the demands of everyday living to pray and meditate.

Our children need to have a place to go that is theirs, and theirs alone. Also, they need to respect the right of their parents to have private time. People who are able to be alone without being lonely have a healthy outlook on living.

Jesus was creative. He had a creative approach to problem solving (changing water into wine, using two fish and five loaves to feed thousands). We know, of course, that He was the Creator of the universe, but when He walked on this earth as a man, He had a fascinating aptitude for coming up with new ways of doing things.

Some people may think creativity is the ability to compose a song, paint a picture, or write a book. Raising children to responsible adulthood is a noble achievement in creativity. Ask any parent who has done it!

Jesus was a marvelous storyteller. He taught great truths, captivating His audience with illustrations. His goal for us, of course, was to learn from the stories.

Too many parents have abdicated the role of storyteller to television. "Tell me a story" has been replaced in many of our homes with "Where's the *TV Guide?*" Now we may not all be good storytellers, but most of us can read stories to our children. What better way to spend time with them and build a foundation of Christian values? Educators have discovered that the child who has been read to at an early age usually becomes a better student as he grows older.

Jesus, the perfect God-man, has given us many examples of modeling. Whether we say it as a prayer or a plea, "Jesus, show me," applies to parenthood.

FOUR REASONS TO INSTILL CHRISTIAN STANDARDS TODAY

Many people with high moral values set a good example for their children; they may even be churchgoers, but that does not necessarily mean that their children learn bedrock Christian standards that will enable them to withstand the lashings of life. God gave the guidelines in His Book, and He instructed parents to teach their children "so the next generation would know them" (Psalms 78:6). As I see it, there are four basic reasons we need to instill Christian standards in our kids.

Reason One: *To give our children the priorities of the Scripture.*

Kids today learn a lot about getting to the moon, but very little about getting to Heaven. They can master the intricacies of the computer better than most adults, but do not know how to explore "the depth of the riches of the wisdom and knowledge of God" (Romans 11:33). They may think the Rock of Ages is a new singer.

A recent survey among high school seniors turned up the following results about their knowledge of the Bible: one-half could not name one of the Gospels; some thought the Epistles were the wives of the apostles; some thought Sodom and Gomorrah were husband and wife; others thought that Moses was Jesus' father.

We are rich in Bible teachings today. Unlike a few generations ago when the King James Version of the Bible was the only source for Christian learning (and the greatest revivals in America sprang from the "thees and thous" of its majestic language), now we have children's illustrated Bibles, video tapes, audiocassettes, vacation Bible schools, puppet shows, records, and concerts. This Christian cafeteria is so full of a variety of food that there's no excuse for parents today not to introduce their children to nutritious spiritual food.

Scripture is a priority for instilling Christian standards. Without it, there are only the "value systems" which the public schools are attempting to build into their curricula. I am not being critical of these attempts at teaching moral systems in a secular context, because conscientious teachers are trying to bring some degree of order out of the chaos in our schools; however, Christian standards are more than value systems. "The whole Bible was given to us by inspiration from God and is useful to teach us what is true and to make us realize what is wrong in our lives; it straightens us out and helps us do what is right. It is God's way of making us well prepared at every point, fully equipped to do good to everyone" (2 Timothy 3:16, TLB).

Reason Two: *To give our children the parenting skills they will need.* In Psalm 78, the writer speaks not only of teaching "the next generation" (our children), but "even the children yet to be born." What a surprise! Johnny may be seven years old and Betsy eleven, but we have responsibility for their children, our grandchildren. One of the great preachers of the last generation was Dr. Harry Ironside. In one of his books he wrote:

> I have on my desk an old, old photograph. It is a photograph of my great grandfather who was a farmer in Aberdineshire, Scotland. The photograph is almost faded out with age, though I have tried to keep it covered from the light, because I wanted to have it as long as I might live. People who knew my grandfather told me that he used to

gather all his large family and his many farmhands together at the end
of each day and pray for the salvation and blessing of his children and
his children's children unto the third and fourth generation.

As I look at the grizzled face of that old Scottish farmer, I thank
God for his prayers and for the way He answered them in my life.

We parents may never realize how we are influencing "the children yet to be born." We are so engrossed with the problems of the
present that the outcome of the future is obscured.

If you have read anything about the apostle Paul, you know
that before he met Christ on the Damascus Road he was one of
the worst persecutors of Christians. We might think that his background contributed to his ruthless actions. Not true. Paul had a
godly heritage. When he was holed up in a gloomy dungeon,
awaiting death, he wrote those tremendous letters to Timothy,
the young man who was like a son to him. He told Timothy, "I
serve, as my forefathers did" (2 Timothy 1:3). In his mind, Paul
was thinking back over years past and realizing that he came
from a line of godly people who loved the truth of Jehovah. He
was a brilliant scholar from a heritage of zealous believers in the
God of Israel.

Paul was in Jerusalem, telling the people there about the Lord
Jesus when the devout Jews of the city seized him with the intent
to kill him. He was taking a brutal lashing when the commander of
the Roman troops heard there was riot going on and led his squad
down to the temple to arrest Paul before he was beaten to death.
The crowd became so violent that the Roman soldiers had to pick
Paul up and carry him. It was a miracle that Paul was able to quiet
the gang who were out to kill him and stand on the "courthouse"
steps and tell them, "I am a Jew, born in Tarsus of Cilicia, but
brought up in this city. Under Gamaliel I was thoroughly trained
in the law of our fathers and was just as zealous for God as any of
you are today" (Acts 22:3).

What he was saying was that he came from a group of ancestors
who were sincere and godly, according to the knowledge they had
of God. When Paul was converted, he still substantially worshiped
the same God as that of such Old Testament believers as Abraham
and David. But now he worshiped in the name of Christ. He knew
that Christ was the Messiah promised to his forefathers.

A Jew's conversion today is not an act of disloyalty to his forefathers. Rather, it is the fulfillment of his forefathers' faith and

hopes and dreams. Paul was deeply conscious of the powerful influences that had shaped his own destiny.

In many ways, Paul was given parenting skills by his heritage. Although he was probably never an earthly father, he was a spiritual father to many, particularly Timothy.

Among the first believers in Jesus Christ were two godly women, grandmother Lois and her daughter, Eunice. These two wonderful women had been teaching their grandson and son, Timothy, the Word of God since he was a little child. Timothy's real father was probably not a believer, and we don't know much about him, except that Timothy came from a divided home. However, as his spiritual father, Paul made up to him what he had lost by not having a godly father. The bond between Paul and Timothy was closer than the ties of a natural relationship.

Many young people who have been called out of a partially godless home have found a common faith in the true family of God. In the case of Timothy, Lois passed on parenting skills to Eunice, and Eunice to Timothy.

The Bible does not teach that the faith of a parent can save a child, but it does teach that the child will imbibe the spirit of faith which his parents held. Grace is not inherited; each individual has to be born again, no matter how pious and devoted his parents are. But let's not forget that all of us influence family relationships.

Yes, we have a responsibility to our children and to their children, born or yet to be born. Dale Evans Rogers said, "In all the reams that have been written on families, parenting, and marriage, grandparents are generally ignored. I'm here to shout, 'Hey, we're important.'"[4]

Like Paul and Timothy, we are debtors to the generations that lived before us; we do not live on an isolated island, "doing our own thing." But the big question is: why do we see so many from so-called Christian homes reacting against the faith of the fathers instead of following it? Why do some who grow up in Christian homes with all the same advantages as Paul and Timothy turn from the faith? If we are to affect our unborn grandchildren, our faith needs to be contagious. I can think of four ways this contagion can be spread.

First, our faith must be authentic. I have talked with hundreds of young people who have rejected the faith and the consistent note I hear is, "My parents talked the faith, but they just didn't live it." I'm not talking about after-dinner faith, daily devotions, or a chapter a day. In Timothy's day, just as in ours, the educated men embraced pagan faiths, keeping up an outward display of their beliefs because of custom or family tradition—or because they thought religion was a positive influence in society. *Religion* has always been the pietistic term men have used in their attempt to describe a moral (or amoral) system. The non-Christian can call himself "religious" and not be questioned. Today we seem to hear more about being "spiritual," which is a tag used to cover a spectrum of beliefs.

Paul described the faith of Timothy, his mother, and his grandmother as "unfeigned" faith. "When I call to remembrance the unfeigned faith that is in thee, which dwelt first in thy grandmother Lois, and thy mother Eunice; and I am persuaded that in thee also." (2 Timothy 1:5, KJV). The word *unfeigned* is not frequently used in modern vernacular, but it means "sincere" or "genuine."

As Christian parents we have the right to expect that our children will be saved if we bring them up knowing the truth about Jesus Christ and His Word, but we must first have authentic or unfeigned faith if it is to be contagious.

Second, our faith must be steadfast and abiding, no matter what life brings our way. Paul also speaks of the faith of Timothy's mother and grandmother as a firm, abiding faith. This is a favorite metaphor of Paul who describes throughout his epistles the indwelling God, the indwelling Spirit, and the indwelling Word. Indwelling faith has staying power. It's there in good times and bad, in happy days and sad, in moments of triumph and days of defeat. Our children will learn more about our faith from the bad times than from the good.

Third, to be contagious our faith must be an aroused faith. William Barclay's definition of a Christian is "A man lost in wonder, love and praise at what God has done for him and aflame with eagerness to tell others what God can do for them . . . ."

A new Christian, one who has just accepted Jesus Christ as Savior and Lord of his life, is an exciting person to be around. He may be shy about his new faith, but his friends remark, "There's something different about him." Or he may be vocal and eager to tell everyone about his new birth. Either way, his enthusiasm is contagious. Certainly Timothy received the type of teaching which aroused his desire to tell others.

Fourth, our faith must be absolute to be contagious. Absolute faith is faith in Jesus Christ; it is a life centered in Christ. *Faith* is an ancient watchword for the apostle Paul. We know what he meant by that well-loved word; he is not talking about mere head knowledge or an acceptance of historical facts. Absolute faith is knowing who Jesus Christ is, without doubting. It is the type of faith Jesus prayed for in John 17:3: "Now this is eternal life: that they may know you, the only true God and Jesus Christ, whom you have sent."

Absolute faith is the only kind of faith that is contagious. You will never communicate an authentic, abiding, arousing faith to your children if you are uncertain about Jesus Christ.

To give our children the parenting skills they need, we must first test ours. Parents, we need to think through the years ahead, past our children to our grandchildren. What do we see? Are we able to imagine the importance of those parenting skills from generation to generation?

Is our faith authentic, abiding, arousing, and absolute?

What about the children? Those who have had the blessing of godly parents, but have trampled it under their feet, have an additional responsibility because of these privileges. Think a moment. When did you last thank your mother or father for blessing your life? The telephone companies may print heartwarming advertisements in magazines, showing Mother smiling through her tears as she receives that precious call, but a phone call can never replace a letter or a note—or a visit!

Reason Three: *To give them a personal walk with God.* Psalms 78 speaks of the generations passing on faith and "they in turn would tell their children. Then they would put their trust in God" (vv. 6–7).

Granted, we cannot be guaranteed that our children will trust God, but it is our only hope today in this climate of despair. We can give our kids every material desire of their hearts, but without a personal walk with God they will be as secure as a leaky boat in the middle of a stormy sea.

Our children may be given the priorities of Scripture, the parenting skills they need, and have a personal walk with God, but there is one more vital reason for instilling Christian standards in our children.

Reason Four: *To give them the practical key to life.* When we teach our children God's Word, they will learn to put "their trust in God and . . . not forget His deeds but . . . keep His commands" (Psalms 78:7).

Putting Christian standards into practice is the key to life. By keeping God's commandments, we give our children the standards to "walk the talk." Our lives speak louder than the preaching of our words.

I have had this poem in my files for years, and I confess I do not know its author. However, it captures so well the essence of this title:

BY YOUR EXAMPLE

He whipped his boy for lying and his cheeks were flaming red,
And of course there's no denying there was truth in what he said—
That a liar's always hated. But the little fellow knew
That his father often stated many things that were untrue.

He caught the youngster cheating and he sent him up to bed.
And it's useless now repeating all the bitter things he said:
He talked of honor loudly as a lesson to be learned,
And forgot he'd boasted proudly of the cunning tricks he'd turned.

He heard the youngster swearing and he punished him again.
He'd have no boy as daring as to utter words profane.
Yet the youngster could have told him—poor misguided little elf
That it seemed unfair to scold him when he often cursed himself.

All in vain is splendid preaching, and the noble things we say.
All our talk is wasted teaching if we do not lead the way.
We can never by reviewing all the sermons on the shelves,
Keep the younger hands from doing what we often do ourselves.

ANOTHER MYTH: THE GOOD LORD RULES
IN THE CHRISTIAN SCHOOLS

Some parents may believe the answer for Christian training is to find a good Christian school for their children. However, not everyone has either the proximity of a Christian school or the financial ability to send their children to one. And it is a myth to believe the complete answer to teaching Christian values is to be found in a Christian school.

Before I attempt to demythologize Christian education and Christian schools, I need to let you know where I have stood and where I stand today.

I grew up with Christian education. When I was entering the seventh grade, my father began his twenty-five-year term as the President of Cedarville College in Cedarville, Ohio. I will never forget living through the formative years of that school: the sacrifice, the suffering, the frustrated dreams that accompanied the growth of that college from its beginning with 90 students to its present size of 1800. I watched the college grow from infancy and eventually graduated from it in 1963.

After four years at Dallas Theological Seminary and a brief stint as a youth pastor, I had the opportunity to start a church in Fort Wayne, Indiana. In 1972 I founded the Blackhawk Christian School. From its humble beginning as a K–3 elementary school, it has become a very strong Christian grade school and high school with over 400 students enrolled.

Presently I am the chancellor of the 400-student Christian Heritage College and serve on the leadership team of the Christian Unified School District—a unique system of schools that includes four elementary schools, a junior high school, and a high school.

I have not written this to impress anyone, but to give this background because I want you to know as I attack this next myth that I am not an enemy of the Christian school movement. However, I am concerned about some current trends in our Christian schools and believe it's time to take inventory and recognize the subtle deception that takes place when we start to believe that "the good Lord rules in the Christian schools."

In the first place, the Lord does not rule in organizations. He can only rule in people. That's where the problem lies: Christian schools, like Christian churches, are made up of people. Christian schools are not curricula, classrooms, and tuition; Christian schools are teachers, students, administrators, and parents. It is the dynamic force created by those four elements that creates the climate of today's Christian schools.

> **The Lord does not rule in organizations. He can only rule in people.**

My children are going to Christian schools. But one concern I have about the nature of Christian education in our generation is that it is only people in the middle to upper class who can afford to send their children; tuition is so high that parents from most families can't afford it, especially if they have more than one child to educate. Consequently, while Christian schools are trying to combat the problem of secular humanism, by their very financial structure they are supporting materialism.

Also, it is increasingly difficult to find Christian teachers who know their subjects and also model their lives by Christian standards. It can be misleading to kids if teachers are skilled in their subjects, but are not leading the Christian lifestyle. Teachers in secular schools can be excused for moral indiscretions; but if the Christian school teacher is not a good example, the consequences in the lives of young students are more devastating. A teacher in a Christian school needs to be a living curriculum—an example of what he or she teaches.

We cannot afford to put our children in a hot-house environment where they never know how to live with the secular world. Is it any wonder that the church is not reaching the world when most Christians don't know how to relate to unsaved families?

It's a risky thing for me to say, believing as I do in the need for Christian education, but there are some young people who are not strengthened by Christian education. I know a fine young man from a Christian home who is in a secular high school where he is a great witness; his parents do not want their boy taken out of this context for it would deprive him of being involved in a vibrant ministry.

Christian education is caught, not taught. I am very fearful for the unsuspecting parent who commits his child to the Christian school with a sigh of relief and believes the problem of schooling has been solved. I have been around Christian schools long enough to see the drastic results of such faulty reasoning.

For Christian parents who truly want the best for their children, the Christian school may still be the proper alternative, provided that they realize Christian education is experienced, not structured. However, having made some rash statements about the system, let me say that I believe in Christian schools, just as I believe in family devotions, but they are not the final answer.

The answer is so simple, it's profound. It was written over nineteen hundred years ago as a warning to a church that was listening to false teaching. "For God's secret plan, now at last made known, is Christ himself. In Him lie hidden all the mighty, untapped treasures of wisdom and knowledge. . . . Let your roots grow down into Him and draw up nourishment from Him. See that you go on growing in the Lord, and become strong and vigorous in the truth you were taught" (Colossians 2:2, 7, TLB).

I believe in the worth of regular times of prayer and worship in a family. However, Christ-centered family worship should be the very fabric of our lives, woven into moments that are not strictly scheduled. We have found that some of the optimal times for sharing God's love are during vacation trips, when the whole family is together in the car, or during holidays when rituals and family traditions are established. A family may sit around the Christmas tree on Christmas Eve and tell what Jesus means to each one of them, or have a special "company" dinner once a week, followed by sharing the blessings in their lives. These times may be even more valuable than the "chapter a day."

Building memories is like investing in antiques; it's an investment that can only appreciate with the passage of time.

MYTH SIX

Read a Book and
Raise a Child

When we had our first child I knew a great deal about the subject of discipline. During my college and seminary years, I had observed examples of poor discipline and knew I would not make the same mistakes. I could have offered good advice on what to do when a child had a tantrum, or sulked, or was sassy. I was so confident in my parenting abilities, that without too much encouragement, I probably could have written a book on how to raise a child. However, after the next three children arrived, I soon realized I didn't have all the answers. In fact, I began to realize I would never graduate from the School of Fatherhood. In order to survive, I would have to be a perpetual student.

I have read most of the popular experts on child-raising, from Spock to Dobson. I must confess there are many facets of the subject that baffle me. Perhaps by the time I'm a grandparent I'll begin to understand why some theories work and others bomb, why child-raising instruction swings on a cultural or social pendulum, and why entire generations of kids are raised by some new idea or testing method.

Of all the challenges that raising a family offers us, discipline may well provoke the most discussion and the greatest differences of opinion. To spank or not to spank, to err on the side of strictness or permissiveness, to be firm or remain flexible—all of these facets of discipline have generated untold numbers of "how to" books.

With all respect to the professionals involved in child psychology and psychiatry, we need to ask the question, "Are we really doing any better job of raising our children with these books than our grandparents did without them?" We cannot allow ourselves to believe that we will automatically find all the answers to raising a perfect child by reading a book, present book included.

Child discipline is simple: it's a matter of knowing which end of the child to pat—and when. Having pronounced those sage words, I am reminded of the words many of us have used when disciplining our children: "This hurts me more than it hurts you." Sincerely said by most parents when applying what they consider more severe disciplinary methods, this phrase is not believed by their offspring until they are grown and have children of their own. Likewise, you may find it difficult to believe that there's anything about child discipline that could be simple.

Just when we think we've discovered the best approach to a problem, we discover our kids haven't read the same theory. Even parents don't agree on disciplinary methods.

How should we react to this scene, for instance? It's 9 P.M. and ten-year-old Jimmy has planted himself firmly in front of the television set, vowing not to move. It's his bedtime, but it's Saturday night and he wants to see the horror movie scheduled to begin momentarily. Jimmy's mother is convinced he should be going to bed now. Right now! As the two of them struggle verbally, Jimmy's father interrupts, "I don't see what the big deal is. If he wants to see this movie so badly, let him. He doesn't have to go to school tomorrow."

Mother insists he should go to bed. Father says they should stop being so inflexible, so strict. As they are locked in debate, Jimmy watches the TV, wondering if it will stay on or off.

As *Parents* magazine states,

Parents today continually question whether their decisions place them on the strict or permissive side of some imaginary dividing line. No parent really wants to tread too far in either direction. With the ever increasing sophistication of their children's world, parents not only face more decisions, but also more difficult ones. Although the consequences of being too strict or too permissive are unclear, many feel strictness leads to unhappy, rigid children and permissiveness to uncontrollable kids.[1]

KEEPING OUR BALANCE IN A TEETER-TOTTER WORLD

Anyone who speaks out on the subject of discipline risks as much criticism as a political candidate. There are so many conflicting voices, even in the evangelical world, that it's too easy to add another theory that may or may not work. Giving advice is a thankless task; if you want people to notice your faults, start passing out your opinions.

The subject of child discipline is one which can even create guilt problems for parents who have already raised their children. They may be led to believe that they have made mistakes which will affect their progenies' personalities forever. Many of us look at the results of our parenting efforts and wonder if we should have followed some checklist on "Five Things to Do after Spanking" or "Four Ideas on How to Treat Your Teens." On the other hand, the thought of changing course in midstream is equally frustrating. When we're in the middle of the priority years for parental discipline we don't want to be told to stop what we're doing because it's wrong. This is frustrating for kids as well as parents. If we parents are to keep our balance in this teeter-totter world, we can't agonize over what others say nor cancel what we have already done. Yesterday's mistakes are today's lessons.

Discipline is not an action, but an atmosphere. Discipline is not a packaged plan; it's a personal plan. For that reason, I do not intend to give a prescription for disciplining your children. Instead, I want to point out principles that have survived for generations of parents. I believe that Scripture is the foundation for understanding any subject, but we should not overlook the perspective of history and culture as well.

> Discipline is not an action, but an atmosphere.
> Discipline is not a packaged plan; it's a personal plan.

Child-rearing (an appropriate term for the subject of discipline) is like education, politics, or fashion; popular views swing from one extreme to another as action demands reaction. For example, Dr. Benjamin Spock led us through the freedom-without-much-discipline era of the '40s and '50s; many children of that time were raised with little self-control and responsibility. However, Spock was blamed for more than he deserved, for it was also a time of war, separations, and an attempt to return to normalcy. Then came the turbulence of the '60s, and the pendulum began to swing the opposite direction. The irresponsible actions of many young people, who relied on drugs and rioting to express their views, resulted in a counteraction on the part of many Bible-believing Christians. One of the most positive additions to Christian thinking was Dr. James Dobson and his book *Dare to Discipline.* He brought a perspective to the subject which was not an overreaction.

The swing of the pendulum away from permissiveness, however, has knocked some Christians into an anti-psychology camp. They have branded psychology as unscriptural and labeled everyone in the profession with one sweep of black paint. This is very unfortunate. I believe child development and psychology are worthy of study and should not be disregarded. Dr. Gene Getz of Dallas Theological Seminary, writing about behavioral problems in children, such as insecurity, anger and hostility, sensitiveness, perfectionism, and sexual disturbance, said, "All of these—and many others—can often be traced back to inappropriate approaches to child discipline. No wonder secular psychologists react against some parental "Christian" tactics. What is even more tragic, some secularists reject Christianity per se because Christians have inappropriately interpreted and applied Scripture in the area of child discipline."[2]

Consequently, we must look to biblical principles, but keep in mind the age, temperament, and environment of a child when considering the various methods of training. Child psychology has taught that children, particularly very young ones, go through certain phases; these are natural and a part of growing and testing. It is what is called a "natural bent." Some Christians, however, classify this God-given need to learn as the "old sin nature" or the "old self will" that must be broken. But to attribute every wrong-doing to the work of the devil is to ignore some of the phases which are common to growing up.

Sometimes when we're involved in disciplining our children we can be knocked off balance by the unexpected. I once heard the story about a little boy who was outside playing while his mother was conducting a Bible study. In the middle of the study he plunged into the living room and announced that there was a lion in the backyard. His mother, chagrined because of the interruption and her son's exaggeration, said, "Johnny, you know there isn't a lion in the backyard. Now you run out and play and leave us alone until we're finished with our study."

"No, Mommy," he panted, "there really is a lion in the back-yard. You gotta come and see."

Reluctantly, the mother walked over to the window and looked out. There was the biggest, yellowest, furriest cat you can imagine. She turned to Johnny and said, "Now you know the difference between a cat and a lion, and you know that isn't a lion in the yard. You march right up to your room and think about that fib."

Realizing she had a captive audience of women in her Bible study, she added, "And while you're up there, tell God what you've done."

With his head bowed, he went upstairs. He was only gone about five minutes when he came back into the room. One of the women asked, "Well, Johnny, did you think about what you did?"

"Yes'm, I did."

"Did you tell God what you said?"

"Yup."

"And what did God say?"

"God said the first time he saw that cat, He thought it was a lion, too."

How could Johnny's mother discipline him after such imaginary logic?

TO LOVE IS TO DISCIPLINE

A young father was working at home when his dad came over to see the new baby. "Aren't you going to do anything about your boy? He's cryin'!" Grandpa said.

The new father patiently explained that if he did something each time the baby cried, the child would be spoiled. After all, he reasoned, he knew the books, and presumably his dad didn't.

"You don't discipline a cryin' baby; you find out the problem. All seven of my kids weren't disciplined until they understood what they were doin'. When the Good Book talks about 'trainin' up a child in the way he should go,' it means you gotta consider how old he is," Grandpa said, giving free advice not always appreciated by a younger generation.

As his child grew, the younger man listened with indulgence to Grandpa's advice about discipline. The baby who had been allowed to cry was older, and new theories on discipline were being expounded by child behavior experts. By the time the child was in kindergarten, he had been allowed to do what he pleased, with very little parental restraints. "Give him his space; don't place too many restrictions upon him," said the father. Grandpa, observing his grandchild's behavior, would mumble, "The Good Book says 'spare the rod and spoil the child.'" But Grandpa hadn't read the latest books.

Years later, after earning a doctor's degree in psychology, the younger man wasn't as sure of himself as he had been as a new father. He had been subjected to so many theories on child-rearing that he began to wonder how the seven children in his family had been treated with any kind of consistency. He realized that his dad had followed a guide which doesn't change: the Bible. Any new concept that came along was evaluated according to Biblical standards.

But psychology is not the real problem here. Psychology is actually consistent with the Bible in teaching that a child should be loved for what he is, not for what he does, just as God loves us for what we are, not for what we do. The problem comes when parents confuse love with license and permissiveness. For just as God disciplines those He loves, so true love means disciplining at the age and understanding level of an individual.

God wants His children to walk the right path, just as we want our children to have the joy and confidence of traveling life's path with assurance. I can remember when we lived in Indiana, taking the hands of our children as we slipped on icy sidewalks. If I could help it, I wanted them to avoid some of the bumps and scars they would receive if they went alone. The Bible's description of God's helping His children to walk the right path begins when He was leading the Israelites through the wilderness. "Know then in your heart that as a man disciplines his son, so the Lord your God disciplines you. Observe the commands of the Lord your God, walking in His ways and revering Him" (Deuteronomy 8:5–6). Since God disciplines His children so that they will walk in His ways, we must discipline our children so they will walk the right path.

THE GOOD NEWS IS
POSITIVE DISCIPLINE

Discipline is sometimes confused with punishment. There is a difference. Punishment is done out of frustration and anger, but discipline is done out of love and concern. Anger may be present in discipline, but it's not a parent's primary motivation.

A coach takes his team through disciplined training before the game so that they will know how to play well and play to win. If someone violates a rule or causes unmerited harm to another player, the referee calls a penalty. Likewise, punishment is what takes place when the rules of the family or society are broken.

The first requisite of guiding our kids down the right path is very elementary: we need to know the path ourselves. The Bible has many metaphors about the right path and is our model for consistently disciplining our children. Take, for example, the familiar Twenty-third Psalm. The Psalmist says, "He guides me in the paths of righteousness" (v.3). Visualize the shepherd leading the sheep on safe paths, helping them avoid the brambles that could trap them. Also, when you read, "Your rod and your staff, they comfort me" (v.4), it suggests that the shepherd may use some rough handling on those animals. A jab with a rod is used to pull the strays onto the path, and the crooked staff was designed to hook the animal at its neck or belly and yank it back into line. The shepherd cares for sheep, but he doesn't pet them and say "poor little lamb" when he sees they're going the wrong way.

The Lord disciplines those He loves. How often do we hear, "Why is this happening to me?" Or "What did I ever do to deserve this?" Good news: it's because we're loved! "My son, do not despise the Lord's discipline and do not resent his rebuke, because the Lord disciplines those he loves, as a father the son he delights in" (Proverbs 3:11).

Positive discipline is a warning sign; it's the yellow light that flashes before stop. Why is it that punishment is used so frequently when the positive direction of clear guidelines could prevent some negative results?

In my late teens, I saw an example of negative results that could have been avoided by some positive directions. The incident has frequently reminded me throughout the years of trying to give my kids a warning when trouble is ahead.

> When I was a college student, I traveled during one summer vacation with the official college quartet. One of the members of that quartet was a red-headed pianist named Rich. To say that he kept us loose is to put it mildly. He saw humor in things that passed the rest of us right by.

When we were singing in Fort Wayne, Indiana, on one occasion, Rich pulled a stunt that reminds me now of the way so many families operate in the area of discipline. After working out at the downtown YMCA, we were standing on the corner waiting for the light to change. Rich saw something that all of the rest of us missed. Reconstructing it, after the fact, we all realized what had happened.

Just before the light turned red, a lady driving a late model car had pulled too far forward and was blocking the crosswalk. When she realized what had happened, she put her car in reverse and backed up. What she did next, only Rich had seen. Just before the light turned green, he poked me in the ribs and said, "Watch this," pointing to the woman's car.

Sure enough, just as the signal changed, she stepped on the gas and instead of going forward, she plowed into the car behind her. She had forgotten to put her car back in forward drive. No one was hurt, but we saw a lot of chrome and glass redistributed.

Wouldn't it make sense to warn her before she made that mistake? To this day I don't know why Rich didn't shout at her, but the point is, why do we as parents often say to each other, "watch this" instead of providing the necessary strong guidance to keep our children out of trouble? Mark it down . . . discipline is positive and positive discipline works.[3]

IT HURTS

Whether it's discipline or punishment, I know it hurts the one who is the giver more than the receiver. It hurts to see that look in your child's face which says, "I don't like you." It is painful to be the one who causes the tears or receives the accusations of cruelty. The task of disciplining is overwhelming, tiring, and frustrating. One young mother said, after a difficult day with the children, "I like to take the car and go for a drive; I need to have something in my hands I can control."

In the Book of Hebrews, the writer emphasizes that God disciplines us because He loves us, that fathers discipline children for the same reason, and that none of us ought to treat lightly the discipline from our earthly fathers or our heavenly Father. This is probably one of the most powerful passages on the subject:

"Endure hardship as discipline; God is treating you as sons. For what son is not disciplined by his father? If you are not disciplined (and everyone undergoes discipline), then you are illegitimate children and not true sons. Moreover, we have all had human fathers who disciplined us and we respected them for it. How much more should we submit to the Father of our spirits and live! Our fathers disciplined us for a little while as they thought best; but God disciplines us for our good, that we may share in his holiness. No discipline seems pleasant at the time, but painful. Later on, however, it produces a harvest of righteousness and peace for those who have been trained by it" (Hebrews 12:7–11).

The Lord tells us that discipline is painful, but He also promises a "harvest" or reward for those children who have received good discipline from parents, teachers, leaders, or trainers. Sports is a prime example of what happens with discipline or the lack of it. Take a bunch of flailing, jumping, dizzying seven- to eleven-year-old boys and give them a football coach who has them stand tall and say "Yes, Sir," makes them attend regular practice, teaches them the rules and strategies, and you may have a winning team. Discipline also brings rewards in life as well as in the playing field, the concert stage, the business world, or the kitchen.

TO SPANK OR NOT

Should parents ever spank their children? The Bible says, "yes," and Proverbs, Ephesians, and Hebrews give the principles. This cuts across the grain of many child experts, who believe that a child's mind is like a computer which when fed correct information will come up with the proper behavior. The Bible doesn't teach such an innocent view of children. Contrary to the views of some, there is such a thing as bad behavior in children. Proverbs 22:15 says, "Folly is bound up in the heart of a child, but the rod of discipline will drive it far from him." Some other clear statements are made in Proverbs 29:15, "The rod of correction imparts wisdom, but a child left to itself disgraces his mother."

We admit we cannot go to the Bible and find specific answers to every challenge we have. No place is it written that using the hand to spank is worse than a paddle, or that father is the only one who should spank. However, God has given us a mind and a set of principles; with these, we should be able to put together the puzzle. Following are seven principles of disciplining found in Scripture.

Principle one: *Discipline proves our love.* "If you refuse to discipline your son, it proves you don't love him; for if you love him you will be prompt to punish him" (Proverbs 13:24, TLB).

We've all heard the "spare the rod and spoil the child" adage, but many modern parents believe this is cruel. I admit that there have not been many times I have spanked our children, but I believe the parameters of conduct were drawn so clearly that they knew if they overstepped them there would be consequences.

It's interesting that the number one reason parents give for not spanking is "because we love them too much." Dr. James Dobson in his best seller, *Dare to Discipline,* has written:

> The parent has got to convince himself that discipline is not something that he does to the child, but something he does for the child. His attitude toward the child must be, "I love you too much to let you behave like that."[4]

Principle two: *No child is excused.* "Let God train you, for he is doing what any loving father does for his children. Whoever heard of a son who was never corrected?" (Hebrews 12:8, TLB).

Unfortunately, there are many sons (and daughters) who have never been corrected. Either through misguided love or neglect, they have been allowed to grow up free as unguided missiles. It is love, not anger, nor frustration, nor impatience that should be the motive to move a parent to discipline. No matter how pretty your darling daughter is, nor how smart your son, discipline is proper for them.

Principle three: *Don't wait until it's too late.* "Discipline your son in his early years while there is hope. If you don't you will ruin his life" (Proverbs 19:18, TLB).

A mother came to me and asked when she should begin to discipline her children. "How old are they?" I asked. "They're nine and eleven," she said. She had waited much too long. But when *is* the time to start? I am certainly not advocating spanking a very young child who is between the ages of one and two, unless it is a little swat administered to keep him from hurting himself or others. This is the age when a child is the great imitator. When he sees others doing something, he will most likely try to do it himself, unaware of the hidden dangers. In our environment there are so many areas where he can get in trouble: the light sockets, the cleaning products in the cupboard, the pans on the stove, the open doors that lead outside or to the basement.

We don't need to go through the obstacles to realize that this is the time to make a child's environment as safe as possible so that spankings are minimized. I must say, however, that I find it difficult to rationalize spankings given for broken treasures such as fine crystal when parents leave these items on the coffee table in easy reach of clumsy little hands. Adults can't resist touching pretty things, so how can we expect a little one to keep his hands off a pretty, breakable object? It's far better to keep it out of reach.

Between the ages of two and three, a child identifies with those he loves, and when he feels secure and comfortable with someone, he will want to be like that person. Disciplining children in the first three years of their lives is more like disciplining parents.

Spankings are more effective when a child understands why he is being spanked, and that ability is not usually reached until the ages of three or four. For these small ones, I believe spanking should be the first option, and a scolding the last resort. Too many times, the word *no* becomes such a habit that it becomes meaningless to the child. Just as spankings should be kept to a minimum, so should this word. If you scold too much, the children will push you just short of using the paddle. (Manipulation is the weapon of childhood.) I firmly believe that one of the biggest mistakes parents can make is to punish with the voice instead of the hand.

Principle four: *The right discipline will not hurt your child.* "Withhold not correction from the child; for if thou beatest him with the rod, he shall not die" (Proverbs 23:13, KJV).

Many times I've been told by honest parents that they don't discipline their children because they're afraid they might cause physical harm. We're caught today in that cultural pendulum which has swung from the permissive age of no corporal discipline to the present age of child abuse. We didn't spank our children then because we didn't believe in it; we don't spank them now for fear of extremes. Surely child abuse is one of the worst blights on our society, and I would not minimize its horror. However, the Bible is not speaking of abuse when it speaks of "beating with a rod," although our modern vernacular would imply this interpretation. Proverbs does not recommend brutal beatings, nor is physical punishment the only method of childtraining mentioned. The saying of "spare the rod and spoil the child" is not true in every circumstance.

The child Solomon refers to in this verse is not a young child, but an older youth. The Book of Proverbs is directed to older children and sons in particular. Most of the verses that mention the rod are referring to a severe form of punishment used in Israel for disciplining young men (and older ones, too) who were extremely rebellious in nature.

Dr. Getz said:

> We must conclude that to apply these verses in Proverbs to child-rearing and discipline with very small children, is certainly not what Solomon had in mind. Rather, it seems he was referring to a form of punishment against various crimes that were committed in the Hebrew society. To use these verses to develop a philosophy of child-rearing and discipline in the home has created some unusual behavioral problems in children—and often brings unfortunate criticism from non-Christian counselors who know from experience that this is not an appropriate approach.[5]

So let's understand that "beating with a rod" is not the brutal phrase we might think. That rod could be a ping-pong paddle, a wooden spoon, or a tough hand. It should be applied only to the cushioned undercarriage of a child, never to his face or another part of his body which could be harmed. When parents meet with open defiance, such as "I will not" or "You shut up," it's time for action. The underlying question is "Who's in charge here?" And a firm hand or paddle, justly applied, can usually set the record straight.

If we are honest with ourselves, most of us do an inadequate job of disciplining not because we're concerned we will hurt our children, but because we don't want to be inconvenienced. Laziness is sometimes disguised as patience to make the lazy person feel more virtuous.

I do not advocate painful spankings with belts, hairbrushes, or sticks. Christian parents who resort too quickly to these measures are misinterpreting God's guidelines for parenting. Even a wooden spoon or small paddle could be misused. Caution and moderation should be our guides.

Principle five: *Discipline proceeds in spite of crying.* "Chasten thy son while there is hope, and let not thy soul spare for his crying" (Proverbs 19:18, KJV).

Crying is not a barometer of pain. Our youngest child was way ahead of this proverb. He cried before any discipline was administered; with him, we got the result before the action. On the other hand, I've already told about another member of our family who doesn't cry at the time of discipline, but dissolves when we hug afterwards.

Kids are very resilient. I've seen a lot of little guys like the one who gets knocked down on the soccer field, skins his knees, sprains his wrist, and never makes a sound. But put him over your knee when he oversteps his behavior boundary, and he'll howl up a storm. The principle in this proverb reminds us that tears are not an indication of successful discipline.

Principle six: *Discipline is not for releasing anger.* "Fathers, do not exasperate your children; instead, bring them up in the training and instruction of the Lord" (Ephesians 6:4).

What exasperates our kids? What makes them feel we are grossly unfair? Some parents think that any discipline will make their children angry, but this isn't true. What exasperates them is unjust accusations; unfair punishment; and nagging, sarcasm, or short-fused anger. "Provoke not your children to wrath," the King James version says. We provoke when we're on their case all the time. The easiest way to separate us from our children is to use sarcasm or snide remarks about their appearance or behavior, particularly in front of others. We exasperate our children by imposing punishment for one child and ignoring bad behavior in another. If we spank our children because we're irritated, or nag to release our own frustrations, we will be "provoking."

It's not hard to understand the mother who says, "The kids were driving me crazy, so I spanked them soundly. It didn't seem to help them, but it certainly did me a lot of good."

Driven by circumstances at work, physical ailments, or some other distress, either internal or external, we often take out our feelings on the most vulnerable people around us. And many times those are the ones we love the most. This tendency reminds me of a scene from an old Jimmy Stewart movie called "It's a Wonderful Life." Stewart was the father who had come to the end of his rope. His business was failing, his friends had turned against him, and his dreams had been dashed. He went home to his wife and children and vented his frustrations on them in a tirade of unjust actions. By the time he stomped out of the room, his family was in tears and he had made himself more miserable than before. Many of us could relate to that scene, but more of us can remember the times we accused our kids before hearing the whole story, or punished one child more severely than another. When children see

injustice they become exasperated. It's not an easy task for parents
to issue discipline fairly, but whoever promised it would be easy?
We only know it's worth it.

Principle seven: *Discipline prepares for life's greatest decision.*
"Punish him with the rod and save his soul from death" (Proverbs
23:14).

Coming to Christ has no age restrictions; however, most of the
decisions are made in the early years and many as a result of
growing up in a Christian home where discipline is practiced.
Parents who teach their children love by caring enough to confront them with their sins teach them about their heavenly Father
who does the same.

Our ultimate goal as Christian parents is to know that our children are believers in Jesus Christ and that they are saved from
spiritual death.

DO WE REALLY
UNDERSTAND DISCIPLINE?

The word *discipline* comes from the Greek word meaning
"disciple." The disciples were learners and pupils; consequently,
discipline is a process by which people learn what is acceptable
and desirable. If a child is taught self-control early enough in life,
there will probably be no occasion for stern whippings, such as
Proverbs describes for older youth.

If spanking is necessary, the important thing is for the hugs to
follow the spanks. When it is over, the one who administers the
punishment (not the other parent) should be the one to soothe the
injured feelings. Then the reason for the punishment should be
repeated and the way to avoid future clashes should be made
clear. No matter what manner of tears, stony silence, or pouty
looks is evident, one way to begin is, "Okay, honey, do you understand why I spanked you?" When the unacceptable conduct is
explained and the consequences understood, then it's time to forgive and forget. Urge your child to pray and ask God's forgiveness
and explain that spankings don't remove or forgive sin, only Jesus
can do that.

What if you discipline, or administer a spanking, and your child will not make up with you afterwards? Suppose your hugs are rejected, your hands are pushed away, what then? My friend Gary Smalley calls this a *closed spirit*: "When a child resists affection—if you touch his hand and it's cold and limp, or if you put your arm around her and she turns her back, shrugs you off and avoids conversation—that usually means the spirit is closing."[6]

Smalley also gives five steps he has successfully used to reopen a child's spirit. First, become tender-hearted. By the tone of your voice and your body language, convey gentleness and tenderness. Second, increase your understanding of the pain your child has after the discipline or punishment. Take time for both of you to cool off. Third, if your attitude was wrong, admit it. "I didn't understand and I flew off the handle." Fourth, attempt to touch, to reach out with your arms. Fifth, seek forgiveness from the one offended.[7]

Those may sound like I'm playing the "rules game," by giving those steps, but if we examine the Lord's Prayer, we'll discover that He already spelled out the principles for forgiving our trespasses, as we forgive those who trespass against us.

One last thought before we move on: spankings should be done in private, so that the child will not lose his self-respect in front of others. Now we'll close the door on the subject of spanking and consider more positive means of discipline.

THE POWER OF PRAISE

Everyone needs positive reinforcement for healthy emotional growth.

It's natural to wither with criticism and blossom with encouragement. But as parents we must guard against using flattery and bribery with our children instead of praise and rewards. Gold stars should not be added to the chart on the wall unless they have been faithfully earned. However, when special goals are reached and rewards have been promised, be sure to carry out your promises. Nothing is so hollow to a child as a promise not fulfilled.

In recent years there has been a secular philosophy called "Parent Effectiveness Training," or P.E.T., which is a "no win—no lose" approach to parent-child relationships. According to this idea, conflicts are solved by the parent buying the child's behavior. "If you do this for me—then I'll do this for you." It is not reward for tasks well done, but bribery for good behavior. The idea espoused in P.E.T., which became a national movement in the late 1970s and continues into the '80s, is that children can be the authority over their own behavior. Children, according to P.E.T. advocates, resent parents who have power over them. Therefore, parents are urged to search for creative, new nonpower methods that all adults can use with children and youth. This avoids what P.E.T. advocates see as dangers that result from leaving the decision for the best interests of children with parents. Does this idea meet with biblical standards? No, it is in direct conflict with the scripture which says, "You children must always obey your fathers and mothers, for that pleases the Lord" (Colossians 3:20, TLB).

The responsibility for training and discipline is first with the Lord, then with parents. Teachers, baby-sitters, and meddling neighbors are not our children's keepers. We should not expect them to do what is our job.

Discipline can take many forms—denial of privileges, holding back the use of a special possession, or isolation for a short period of time—but praise and rewards for a job well done is often the most effective approach for training our children and building healthy self-esteem. A Proverb reminds us, "Pleasant words are a honeycomb, sweet to the soul and healing to the bones" (16:24).

DON'T GIVE UP

Some parents become so frustrated with the behavior of their child that they look back on times when they were "too easy" and think, *We've made so many mistakes; I don't think he'll ever straighten up.* Parents often become discouraged by the defiant, resistant, disobedient behavior of their children. With some strong-willed children, discipline can be both mind-consuming and time-consuming. But parents must avoid the tendency to nag, yell, lecture, shame, threaten, criticize, or tease. It does no good. In fact, such behavior on the part of parents shows lack of respect for the child, which is a trait we do not want to model for our kids.

Our goal as parents is to lead our children through the years of parental discipline to the goal of self-discipline, which will enable our children to lead loving and happy lives with others.

Our goal as parents is to lead our children through the years of parental discipline to the goal of self-discipline.

READ THE RIGHT BOOK
AND RAISE A CHILD

I have a library full of books on raising children. If you were to come in and choose one off the shelf, the book you read may be sound psychologically, written skillfully, and explained logically. More than likely, it would be the wisdom of one person or the theory of one school. But the book I recommend to read is the Bible, and the best chapter on the subject of discipline is probably Hebrews 12, which gives us guidelines we need to constantly review.

Whenever God gives us a tough assignment, we need to praise Him that He cares for us as a child. The Living Bible says: "And have you quite forgotten the encouraging words God spoke to you, his child? He said, 'My son, don't be angry when the Lord punishes you. Don't be discouraged when he has to show you where you are wrong. For when he punishes you, it proves that he loves you. When he whips you it proves you are really his child" (Hebrews 12:5–6).

We need to remind ourselves, not just our children, that discipline proves love. God never tires of disciplining us; He will not give up on us. However, if we want an abundant life, if we want to really live, not just exist, we are told that even if it is painful, discipline turns mere existence into living. "Since we respect our fathers here on earth, though they punish us, should we not all the more cheerfully submit to God's training so that we can begin really to live?" (Hebrews 12:9, TLB).

If we can remember through the pain that it is for the purpose of an abundant life, a life full of joy and happiness, we will be able to smile at the end of the tears. Disciplining kids is an adrenaline-charged procedure; but God says, "Take a new grip with your tired hands, stand firm on your shaky legs, and mark out a straight, smooth path for your feet so that those who follow you, though weak and lame, will not fall and hurt themselves, but become strong" (Hebrews 12:12, TLB).

No other book gives us the encouragement and guidance for this wonderful privilege of parenthood than our Father's Book!

MYTH SEVEN

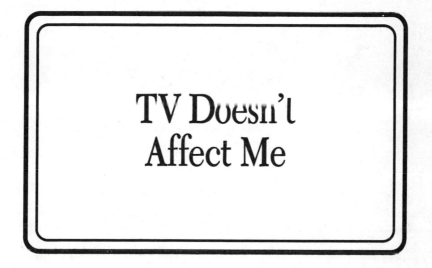

TV Doesn't
Affect Me

When television was a baby, one of its first stars was Jackie Gleason, who would say, as he executed a little shuffle, "And . . . awaaay we go!" A generation later, television has become the most popular mass communications medium in history. It can be used by either the powers for good or the powers for evil to influence millions of humans by just a flick of the dial. But which side is winning this battle for the minds?

Voices are being raised today against the violence, immorality, and distortions of reality seen on the TV screen. If you ask concerned parents about the influence television has on them or their children, you may find many of them a little defensive: "We don't watch TV very much . . . and when we do, we're very selective. We watch the ball games and the news, and the kids have certain programs we allow them to see, but otherwise it's not on much. TV doesn't really affect us."

The eye in the cabinet looks into the family room or living room, the hotel, or bar, and winks knowingly at the naiveté of human beings. It knows that the images it shows are never neutral. Every program teaches something; television has become the most pervasive means of influence in America today. It is a myth to think we are immune to the mental and moral manipulation of TV programming and advertising. In many households today, the easiest way to get a kid's attention is to stand in front of the TV set.

> It is a myth to think we are immune to the mental and moral manipulation of TV programing and advertising.

121

IT'S NOT ALL BAD

When we begin to expose the flaws of TV, one of the first things we hear is, "There's a lot of good stuff on TV." True. Likewise we can go into a fast food restaurant and buy a glass of milk, and, perhaps, be fortunate enough to find a salad bar stocked with fresh vegetables. The steady fare on the menu, however, consists of junk food soaked in fat, salt, and excess calories. The same is true with the standard TV menu. It feeds our minds while it entertains with less offensive fare, but it can lead us into a diet of killer food.

The critics don't agree. Some say that television has made us more aware of the world around us. It has given us the chance to see what is happening in other countries. Documentaries provide us with insights into the problems of the underdeveloped nations, the plight of the less fortunate, and the personalities of people we would never be able to meet. Veteran broadcaster Eric Sevareid says:

> On balance, TV is better for us than bad for us. When Gutenberg printed the Bible, people thought that invention would put bad ideas in people's heads. They thought the typewriter would destroy the muse, that movies would destroy legitimate theater, that radio would destroy newspapers, and that TV would destroy everything. But it doesn't happen that way.[1]

Television is applauded for boosting worthwhile causes. It allows fund-raising opportunities for organizations, such as Muscular Dystrophy and Easter Seals. Millions of children have been taught the alphabet and simple mathematics by educational series. From "Kukla, Fran, and Ollie," who nurtured today's young parents, to "Sesame Street" for their children, there have been wholesome, entertaining influences.

With television, invalids and the elderly have a source of entertainment to fill lonely hours. Anyone who has visited a convalescent hospital or retirement home will discover TV sets in constant use in the recreation hall and many bedrooms. We would be insensitive if we did not recognize the therapy it provides.

TV defenders say it makes us laugh, gives us news, takes us to sporting events all over the world, and provides us with theater we couldn't afford to attend. It allows Billy Graham to be the evangelist more people have seen than any other Christian in the world's history. I am not on a campaign to ban television. Let's face it; it's here to stay, but I think we have the power and the ability to control it, and we have a responsibility to exercise that power.

OUR LOVE-HATE
RELATIONSHIP

We are told that television is still in its infancy—which explains why you have to get up so often and "change" it. TV worries parents, distracts children, and challenges the corporate moguls. We can't live with it and we can't live without it. It's truly a love-hate relationship.

Parents magazine conducted a national telephone survey of parents and their opinions about television. Of those polled, 60 percent said that most TV programs are not worth watching; 72 percent said there is too much violence.[2]

People will differ on what they believe is worth watching, but there's no denying that there is too much violence. According to this survey, parents pass down their viewing habits to their children. Dr. Gerbner, dean of the School of Communications at the University of Pennsylvania, said, "Viewing is a ritual. We call it a new religion; it's something that you're born into. Children develop viewing habits in the first four, five, or six years of life. Of course, that means essentially that parents set an example not by what they say, but by what they do."[3]

In case you haven't heard, a child's definition of a torture chamber is a living room or den without a TV set. A seven-year-old boy told his mother, "I don't want to go to Grandma's house. She can only get two channels."

Mom and Dad are often more concerned about what the kids are viewing on TV than they are about their own viewing habits. In the *Parents* magazine survey I cited earlier, 28 percent of the parents said they watch too much TV; 61 percent said they watch the right amount. But among the same parents, 40 percent said their children (who averaged over two hours of viewing on a given evening) watch too much TV.

Dr. John Condry, director of the Human Development and Television Research Lab at Cornell University, said, "Television is an uncontrolled part of the culture. Parents are worried about the effect it's having, but they don't know what to do about it."[4]

MASS HYPNOSES

The average television set is on for more than seven hours every day. Many Americans invest more time with television than with their jobs. By the time most students graduate from high school, they will have spent more time watching TV than in any other activity, except sleeping. They will have witnessed 18,000 murders and watched 350,000 commercials.

Television is the focal point of our attention. We arrange our furniture around it, eat our meals in front of it, and make our appointments to accommodate it.

This mesmerizing teacher in our living room is effective, but the curriculum is decided by a few hundred writers and producers in New York and Hollywood who control the medium and give us their ideas about what life is all about.

The value systems being taught to captive students, curled on the couch or sprawled on the floor for hours at a time, are warped. Although most of us would say *violence* is the most negative value in prime time, we overlook other flaws that permeate the airwaves, such as the approval of deceit. Again and again the message being conveyed is that it's permissible to lie if you can get away with it. Even the story lines in some of the funniest comedies are built upon masking the truth.

Most of us fail to realize how much commercials influence value systems. With radio we used to hear, "And now a word from our sponsors." With television, the commercials are inserted into the drama, comedy, sports, or news with little warning. And like sour grapes in the center of the bunch, they're in our mouth before we know what's happened.

Commercial television is not as interested in entertaining or elevating minds as it is in arousing desires for the sponsors' products. But in many ways we are grateful for this freedom when we consider the propaganda possibilities in state-owned television. We are given our choices in a free-market economy, as long as the advertising is tasteful and the products are fairly represented.

Children are the captive audiences for advertising sponsors. The desires of young viewers are stimulated to a fever pitch to own the latest doll or the newest robot. Toy products used to be spin-offs from characters in kiddie entertainments, such as Mickey Mouse dolls and Dick Tracy rings. However, toy manufacturers and producers of children's programs began to realize they could join forces to produce entire "kidvid" shows around existing lines of playthings. Now the programs themselves became full commercials for the casts of toys. *Newsweek* magazine commented:

> As might be expected, kidvid guardians regard the trend with something less than goggle-eyed rapture. The main problem, they contend, is that the typical viewers of toy-inspired shows are too young to distinguish between the programming and the propaganda, the storytelling and the selling. "It's not clear to small children when the ad begins and ends," says S. Norman Sherry, a member of the American Academy of Pediatrics.[5]

Children are not able to grasp that television may be like a funhouse mirror, distorting life to amuse them; instead, they see it as a picture of reality. More serious are the consequences from the distortions in the "magic window" which teach that violence is the key to power. One little boy said he wanted to be like wrestler Hulk Hogan "because he hurts people, and then they do what he wants."[6]

According to research published by Denver Conservative Baptist Seminary in 1986, it is interesting to note that one set of figures shows eight out of every ten television programs contain violence. In prime time we can watch about eight violent acts an hour; however, children's cartoons are much worse, averaging a violent episode every two minutes. By the age of fifteen, a teenager has seen more death and destruction on television than a soldier who has been through a war.

Broadcasters and producers have been trying to gain more public and parental acceptance of programs by adding a moral, like the teaching methods in Aesop's fables. "They have added moralistic messages tacked on at the end of violent cartoon shows, for example, in an attempt to convince their audience that the programs do have some redeeming social value. However, researchers such as Jerome L. Singer, Ph.D., at Yale University claim that the kids watching the shows often don't get that message. What they pick up on is the violence."[7]

If might is right, then sex is next as the number two distortion. The message being conveyed on the TV screen is that sex does not mean commitment (how often have you seen a couple celebrate their silver or golden wedding anniversary in a teledrama?). Instead, sex outside of marriage is seen as great fun or a perpetual

tease. Sex sells products to make us more desirable, promises pleasures without obligations, and turns God's beautiful blessing into a
snicker. As someone has said, "Most of us have seen TV grow from
infancy to adultery."

Television and the movies have forced us to say farewell to the
Age of Innocence. Values have been eroded in a steady progression,
lessening our shock capabilities until we accept the next obscenity
and the increasing vulgarity with a lessening sense of indignation.
Prime-time television offers new values to attack the old. The spiritual battle has been so gradual that some of us have forgotten how
intense the war is. Why have the dull life of commitment, friendship, service to others when we can live in the fast lane with glamorous men and women, flashy cars, and sexy clothes?

The Bible says, "Avoid godless chatter, because those who in-
dulge in it will become more and more ungodly" (2 Timothy 2:16).
It begins with just one slip at a time until we are caught in an
avalanche.

SCRATCHES ON THE TV TRAY

A few years ago the statistics on "Johnny Can't Read" jarred
educators and parents. The implications were for a generation of
functional illiterates. It's no news that Johnny can't write, either.
The advent of television brought a new tool for education, as well as
a stumbling block. This combination curse-blessing is reaping the
dismal results in student performance levels. In a recent publication
of *A Nation at Risk,* The National Council on Excellence in Education raised serious questions about the educational system in our
country. This report (which is available from the U.S. Government
Printing Office, Washington, DC, 20402 for $4.50), says 23 million
American adults are functionally illiterate; nearly 40 percent of seventeen-year-olds cannot draw inferences from written material;
only 20 percent can write a persuasive essay. TV is not completely to
blame for these frightening trends, but it is a major contributor.

Many kids con their parents into allowing them to do their
homework while watching television. TV trays or reasonable fac-
similes are used for doing assignments, and sometimes the grades
are good enough so Mom and Dad give in, although their gut-level
feelings might be that it is counterproductive. There are some

valid reasons to back up those feelings. "Most educators believe that even though children might get the homework done while watching TV, the division of attention prevents them from learning as effectively as when the television is turned off. If a student's goal is to simply 'do homework,' television does not interfere. If his goal is to learn, turn it off."[8]

> "If a student's goal is to simply 'do homework,' television does not interfere. If his goal is to learn, turn it off."

Reading and writing are inseparable twins. A lot of attention has been given to the sorry reading skills of our youth, but the writing ability is equally poor. The National Assessment of Educational Progress (NAEP) prepared an extensive report on the state of students' writing ability. Nearly 55,000 students participated in this study, so the results are worth our consideration. *Consumers' Research* reported:

> The results provide an overall portrait of the writing achievement of American students in grades 4, 8 and 11. This portrait is not flattering: Most students, majority and minority alike, are unable to write adequately except in response to the simplest of tasks. Although writing performance improves from grade 4 to grade 8— and less dramatically from grade 8 to grade 11—even at grade 11, fewer than one-fourth of the students performed adequately on writing tasks involving skills required for success in academic studies, business or the professions.[9]

What does this mean for the future? Being able to communicate is vital in all relationships, and young Americans need to be equipped with more than "y'know" and "like;" they need a good foundation in the basic skills of their native tongue. The most distressing of the findings in the NAEP report is the difficulty older students had in defending their ideas. "Even at grade 11, relatively few students were able to provide adequate responses to analytic writing tasks, and fewer still were able to muster arguments to persuade others to accept their points of view."[10]

A high school student does not have to be taught how to wangle late hours or the family car, but his ability to compose a letter applying for a job or to use coherent explanations for his viewpoint is abysmal.

At all grade levels, there was a consistent relationship between writing achievement and television. As the number of hours per day of viewing increased, the achievement levels decreased. Good writers are good readers, and the highest achievements were realized for those students who reported reading eleven to fifteen pages a day. At grade eleven, students who reported reading more than twenty pages a day for school and homework had the highest writing ability.

What about eating in front of the TV? After all, that's why those wonderful TV trays were designed. Eating while watching television reinforces the children's dependence upon the electronic tube and may lead to sloppy eating habits. Family conversation is limited to "Where's the salt?" and even the most tastefully prepared dinner is not appreciated. Why should the cook spend time and effort with a nice meal if it is stuffed away between bombings in Beirut and the next episode of "Life in the Fast Lane?"

Who said that TV isn't an effective educational device? No nation in history has ever known as much as we do about detergents and deodorants.

THE SUBTLE BATTLE

Violence, immorality, and twisted values are blaring examples of harm in the tube, but another concern is erosion which takes place in the minds of the viewers. The apostle Paul wrote: "And no wonder, for Satan himself masquerades as an angel of light. It is not surprising, then, if his servants masquerade as servants of righteousness" (2 Corinthians 11:14).

Dr. John Graham, a pastoral psychotherapist, said, "One major side effect of television is that the message-sender acclimates the viewer to the message, slowly breaking down resistance and building up acceptance. In psychological terms, this is called 'systematic desensitization.'"[11]

This is the scene: a viewer watches television from the comfortable, nonthreatening atmosphere of his home. He settles into the easiest chair, or sprawls on the sofa, and images begin to appear on the screen. The pictures are planned to elicit certain emotional responses, such as laughter, tears, sympathy, shock, envy, or desire. Then a commercial interrupts, and he jumps out of the chair to go to the refrigerator. When he hears the program resume, he hurries back to the couch to watch the next scene in the relaxed atmosphere in his living room. The cycle continues: watch the tube, be diverted for a brief time, then back to the next act. This routine begins to desensitize the viewer until ultimately he can view the most disturbing, vulgar scenes without concern. Emotions soon become neutralized until he has reached the "nothing shocks me anymore" mentality.

Television has other side effects that are being researched by many scholars. For instance, studies have been done to indicate that the longer the set is on, the slower the brainwave activity. A person can sit back and have pictures conveyed to him and be totally passive, unaware of the world outside the pictures. A good description for the heavy viewer is "spaced out." Most of us can remember times when we have watched a mini-series (some call these continued sagas "miseries"), and after the final credits, we have staggered to our feet, feeling like zombies. In bed that night, images from the series have flashed across our subconscious, imbedded themselves in our memory banks, and prepared us for the next assault on our minds.

What is our defense in this battle? Moral indignation and continual criticism will not alter the progress of the industry, for good or for evil. The Bible gives us our strategy, as well as our victory: "For our struggle is not against flesh and blood, but against the rulers, against the authorities, against the powers of this dark world and against the spiritual forces of evil in the heavenly realms. Therefore put on the full armor of God, so that when the day of evil comes, you may be able to stand your ground" (Ephesians 6:12–13).

COLD TURKEY

Is there life after the death of a TV? Some people have actually pulled the plug and managed to survive. It's a drastic measure, not recommended by media doctors, but it has been discovered that the patients can live.

One teacher wrote that a seventh-grade student asked her if she had seen a special television show the night before. The teacher replied, "No," and the child was surprised. It was a program high on the viewer rating charts, and it was astonishing that Teacher hadn't watched.

The teacher said, "We don't have a television set, so I seldom see anything on TV."

"Well, whatever do you do?" the puzzled child asked. It was inconceivable that someone didn't own a television.

How does a family without a television fill the evening hours? (Believe it or not, there are some of us who remember those prehistoric days before the advent of television.) The brave woman in the previous story wrote the following explanation about what she and her family do with their evening hours:

> We read. Ed subscribes to three daily newspapers and a score of magazines each month. Every two weeks the children and I go to the library, leaving with a grocery bag filled with books. For hours we sit in companionable contentment, munching apples, playing records and quietly turning the pages, occasionally asking the meaning of a word, or sharing a joke or item of news.
> I read aloud to the children. . . .
> We play music. . . .
> Our cluttered yet comfortable kitchen is the frequent scene of family baking sessions. . . .
> We have games, hobbies and jobs. . . .
> Best of all perhaps, we talk. We plan trips, most of them dreams, although some have come true. We discuss politics and morality and the Bible. We ponder aloud about colleges to attend, jobs to seek, friends to enjoy. We try to be frank, honest, kind and fair in our conversation.
> Recently James, our oldest, was asked what gave him his greatest joy or pleasure in life. Thoughtfully he answered, "Being with my family."[12]

Most of us would probably say, "It's too late for those drastic measures in our family." Or, "We'd go bananas without a TV!" Perhaps the cold turkey approach is an extreme direction we're not willing to take. Thomas Jefferson said, "I cannot live without books," and most of us today would say the same thing about TV. It has reached the point that a person will not have to carry a book to the park, beach, or the airport; he can take the small-screen TV with him for continuous entertainment.

TAMING THE
IDOL IN THE BOX

The prophet Isaiah said, "Shall I bow down to a block of wood?" (Isaiah 44:19).

The power to tame the tiger in the tube is in our hands. I don't hate my TV set; I believe it is a marvelous invention that offers us a world view we cannot perceive from any other media. But it has sneaked up on us so gradually that we need to gain a proper perspective.

When families shut off television for a week or two at a time, the results are predictable: at first it's torture. Then, by the end of the trial period, all sorts of activities have taken the place of TV, and the point has been proven. After a time, however, it's back to the old routine, like the person who goes on a crash diet and then returns to his unhealthy eating habits.

We weren't born addicts. One young mother wrote:

> After sitting for hours on Saturday morning, [the children's] eyes would actually look glazed. When called from the TV, they would be in foul moods. They would angrily stumble away from the couch, looking the way adults do as they leave a movie theater in the middle of the afternoon—disoriented and confused to be in the sunlight again.
>
> The children's TV viewing had slowly, insidiously grown from something I could control to something that was in danger of controlling me.[13]

Her solution was to have the TV dark during the week. It wasn't easy at first; withdrawal pains were severe. She said that one day her third grader had to fill in a chart for a school assignment, telling how many hours of TV he watched each day. His page was blank, and he was so mortified that he confessed later he filled in a fake amount before he would allow anyone to see his paper.

> The mother said, "It is a little strange telling your own friends that your kids don't watch TV at all during the week. For one thing, no one really believes you. They say something like, neither do mine, except for education stations, or neither do mine, except for movies we rent. . . . Or they get very defensive: 'Well, what's wrong with TV?' My answer, honestly, is 'Nothing—unless you have TV addicts in your family.'"[14]

Total withdrawal or partial abstinence may not be the solution for all of us. Instead, we may choose to find our direction by the time-tested method of problem solving. That means we must first admit there is a problem. Second, we must describe the extent and implications of that problem. And third, we must offer a solution, or some solutions.

BACK TO BALANCE

When we look at the priceless children God has given us, we're filled with great expectations for them. By the grace of God, we want them to make a difference in their world, to grow into men and women who will escape from the kingdom of darkness and walk in the light.

We want to nurture their *curiosity.* The normal baby finds the world exciting and inviting; we must not stifle this natural curiosity. As he grows older and begins to ask "why" a dozen times a day, it is a sign of a mind reaching out for knowledge and insight. How stimulating it is to meet a person who is always curious to learn more; such people are interesting at six or at sixty-six.

Dr. Henry Baron, a professor of English at Calvin College, said, "Too many of us allow our children and ourselves to trifle away our time insipidly before silly programs that stifle curiosity, dull the intellect, and stunt the imagination. . . . I know from research studies that after much television viewing even the best minds suffer in their ability to learn."[15]

We want our children to develop a conscience, to become discerning. Therefore, we must find a way to bring before them alternatives to the trash that is spread throughout the media, so that they can enjoy the bright and the beautiful in contrast to the dull and the ugly.

Paul was confined to a Philippian jail when he wrote the positive command, "Finally, brothers, whatever is true, whatever is noble, whatever is right, whatever is pure, whatever is lovely, whatever is admirable—if anything is excellent or praiseworthy—think about such things" (Philippians 4:8). He could not change the circumstances of his imprisonment, but he could control his attitude.

Commitment is another virtue we want to nurture in our children: commitment to the family, commitment to worthwhile goals, and, most of all, commitment to the will of God through Jesus Christ. The subliminal seducers of the mass media also want commitment; the loyalty they are seeking is to their products and their world view of moral and political values. It must be our determination, however, that they do not kidnap our children with kidvid.

Here are ten suggestions that may help us become better parents in regard to television.

1. *Appraise your viewing patterns.* In talking about television with parents I have discovered that many of them don't know the television habits of their home. One of the first things we need to do is to sit down and do a study on when we watch television or what patterns of viewing we have. Just make the list and prepare to study it.

2. *Prepare a list of TV goals.* Basically, there are two reasons why people watch television: one is for information and the other is for recreation. There are many programs that can be watched together as a family that will provide the opportunity for family interaction and the reenforcement of family standards.

3. *Predetermine what you will watch.* Just as impulse spenders may get into trouble financially, so impulse TV watchers usually get into trouble, too. Flipping through the channels, we may catch an unsavory scene we would not want our children to see. Or we may overindulge in a late show at the expense of our mental alertness the next day.

If we decide ahead of time what we will watch and stick to it, we will discover television is back in our control.

4. *Prescribe the amount of time you will spend watching television.* Some families have discovered it is helpful to have no TV on school days. This becomes a part of accepted family life. Others limit television to one hour a day. In our family we let the children choose two programs from the ones we have determined are acceptable. After their programs are over, their viewing time is, too.

5. *Periodically we need a check-up.* We all have a habit of slipping back into old ways.

6. *Protest to the network's stations and sponsors, and commend them for good programs.* It's much easier to have some

postcards handy and dash off a note when a scene, an obscenity, or an immoral concept flashes on the screen than it is to remember to object after the fact. The same is true when we see things we like. We are the consumers, and we have the right and obligation to make our voices heard.

7. *Practice what you preach.* I suppose if any principle has been shouted from these pages more than once, it has been this one. I have awakened in the middle of the night in a sweat, just thinking about how important it is to practice what I preach. As the pages in this book increase, the spotlight on the author seems to get more intense. I submit my fallibility to my readers, while praying for the discernment God has promised.

I admit that Monday night football has had me glued to the screen more than once, but my own obligations and lifestyle have prevented me from becoming a TV addict. However, there is another factor we parents need to take into consideration: if we forbid our children to watch certain programs by sending them to their rooms to read or study, and then leave these programs on for our own enjoyment, we are indulging in duplicity that is hard to explain.

8. *Plan other experiences and activities.* Children usually would prefer to be involved in group activities rather than to be spectators. We have enough spectator sports without becoming a nation of "videots."

9. *Become a part of a community action group.* When we are exposed to something that we feel is offensive, we don't accomplish much by grousing to ourselves. Pick up the phone and call the station. When the switchboard lights start blinking, producers and sponsors take notice.

10. *Pray for wisdom and discernment.* Television cannot be taken casually as an electronic toy to be used for pleasure or education. In this Age of Television, we are being influenced at every level of our lives by what we see and hear on the tube. It is a myth to believe that TV doesn't affect us. With its ability to invade our world with its messages, we need to pray for the wisdom to know how to use it. James 1:5 says, "If any of you lacks wisdom, he should ask God, who gives generously to all without finding fault, and it will be given to him."

If we don't seek God's wisdom, there are many forces seeking our attention with their wisdom. The wonderful minds of our children are being molded. It used to be that parents were able to impart the secrets of the adult world to their children at the proper time in their lives. Television changed that. Now children can learn about sex, power, and the violence of human beings while Mom and Dad are out or uninvolved in what is being seen on the screen.

TV has invaded our world. Will it help our children think about "whatever is true, whatever is noble, whatever is right, whatever is lovely, whatever is admirable" (Philippians 4:8)? That should be our goal.

MYTH EIGHT

Teens Are Trouble

S he's twelve, going on twenty, and I'm dreading the next few years. I guess the thought of living with an adolescent is frightening enough, but soon her brother will be there and we'll have two teenagers in the same house. Good grief, here comes double trouble!"

One mother expressed her sentiments with a resigned sigh, but I wanted to say, "Hold on . . . don't despair . . . who said adolescence and major problems always go together?" I believe this myth has been perpetrated by the exceptions, not the rule. For every headline made by the teenage drug user, runaway, or suicide, there are hundreds of stories about kids who survive those years between childhood and adulthood with only a minimum of trauma. They're the ones who don't make the headlines, but make the team, earn their diplomas, and only drive their parents to distraction once a week.

We do not need to program ourselves or our kids to believe that adolescence is a time of rebellion! Childhood is not all carefree; the middle years are not all destined for mid-life crisis; the elderly are not all senile; teenagers are not all terrors. Why should we allow anyone to be typecast?

The years when our kids are teens can be the very years we parents enjoy the most because they're exciting and fun; just like a roller coaster, we can expect some ups and downs, but eventually we'll step on steady ground again. During this time our emerging adult will experience physical changes and increased responsibilities. That means a certain amount of stress and tension can be expected. But it doesn't mean full-scale rebellion is inevitable. The years are short, the heartaches and triumphs will be frequent, but the ultimate goal is that our children become godly adults. It's like teaching them to swim; we can stand by and coach, but we can't swim for them.

ADOLESCENCE: A TWENTIETH
CENTURY INVENTION

"Parents facing the problems of their teens' adolescence often think these problems have been around for thousands of years. This is not true, however: the phenomenon of adolescence has occurred only during the last century."[1]

When I read that statement by a Christian psychologist, it occurred to me that our age and culture have developed many stereotypes. We box people up in the way we view them and give them labels. I admit I thought *adolescence* was a stage of life that had always been around; however, in over three thousand years of human history, many cultures have considered persons in their early teens to be adults. In past centuries, the age of puberty occurred during the late teens; consequently, there was no period of adolescence; teens were adults before the time of puberty.

One of our young children heard me talking about preteen changes and remarked, "I sure don't want any of that puberty." Whether they like it or not, kids will "get puberty" sooner or later. Over the last hundred years, the age of puberty, which is the beginning of sexual maturity, has been steadily dropping. Children develop at earlier ages in our era because of better diets and health care. Some doctors in the field of human development even say that an increase in light has contributed to this earlier age at which puberty is occurring. It is believed that as we have lighted our homes and our cities, and as our children spend hours in front of bright television screens, sexual and physical development have been accelerated.

Adolescence, then, is considered the years between puberty and adulthood. It is that time of life when the growing individual makes the transition from childhood to adulthood—the period that anthropologists call "rites of passage."

In simpler cultures, initiation into adulthood is usually short; a tattoo, or a change of clothing or hairstyle may be all that's needed to indicate they've been admitted to the adult world. However, in our society, it's not so easy. Today there is a period of five or more years during which physically and sexually mature young people are neither children nor adults. Since they are still dependent economically and legally upon their parents, we call them adolescents. The ages at which one is able to have a job, to vote, to enter military service, to get married have varied so from year to year and from state to state that there is no standard pattern for when adolescence ends and the privileges of adulthood begin.

Among the ancient Hebrews, marriages were common for girls at the age of twelve and for boys at about thirteen. In all probability Mary, the mother of Jesus, was very young when she was betrothed to Joseph. This could mean that Mary was little more than an early teenager when she gave birth to Jesus.

During the Middle Ages the legal marriageable age in most of Europe was twelve. Early marriages were the rule in England during the seventeenth and eighteenth centuries, and the Puritans in America encouraged their children to be married young because they thought it was the best way to avoid premarital sex.

Very early marriages are rare in contemporary Western culture, where marriage is considered one of the determining factors of adult status. In most states it is illegal to be married before eighteen without parental consent.

We can't turn back time, and we wouldn't want to. But it is nevertheless true that trying to steer a sexually mature young person toward responsible adulthood in a sex-saturated culture that emphasizes instant gratification is one of the great challenges for parents with Christian principles.

HURRY UP . . . GROW UP

Somewhere en route to adulthood, millions of kids are missing out on being kids. In low-income families, children have always been forced to grow up early. They need to make money, take over home duties, and raise younger brothers and sisters. Now that kids in middle-class families have single parents and step-families, they, too, are forced into discarding many of the advantages of just being young and carefree.

Psychologist David Elkind, who has met with hundreds of teenagers in private practice, schools, hospitals, and clinics throughout the country, said in an interview, "Everywhere I go, kids feel neglected and unparented. They are mourning a lost childhood and are depressed because they missed something they can never regain. One 12-year-old told me that since he was 6, both his parents have worked, and every morning he has made his own breakfast. He can do it perfectly, but he said—in the plaintive tone I hear so often—'I just wish they would do it for me once in a while.' It would be a sign that he can be a kid now and then, that he doesn't have to be a grown-up all the time."[2]

Teachers and pediatricians tell us that they are seeing in children an increasing number of headaches, bellyaches, sleeplessness, and eating disorders—all of which are chronic symptoms representing stress. (But let's not err on the side of extreme suspicion and think that every time Bill or Patty complain about not feeling well that they are exhibiting childhood stress.)

The hurry-up child is a product of our age, and the trend is snowballing. People are even trying to condition their babies in the womb, and at the infant level, there's the new "superbaby" phenomenon. There's early reading, early math, early computers, early sports, even early beauty contests. Parents have always had high hopes for their kids, but what's new is that preschoolers and preteens are being rushed into the expectations normally reserved for high school seniors.

I read with amazement about the new teachings that are being explored to give children a head start toward the good life of their future dreams. Four-year-old Eric is a star pupil at a computer school where he has mastered spelling words and is currently working on simple graphics. Benjamin is three and a half and is a veteran of swimming, art, gymnastics, and piano classes. Alison is eleven months old and has spent more than half her life working out at the YMCA pool, learning the basics of water survival.

One explanation for this current superbaby phenomena may be that today's new parents, after having survived the 1970s and having their consciousnesses raised, their minds expanded, their assertiveness trained, their bodies firmed, their feelings gotten in touch with, and their competencies expected, entered the '80s ready to change the "I" into "We." And when baby was born, what could be more natural for these same parents than to translate the *can-be adult* into the *can-do baby?*

Anxious to realize the dreams of success they have for their children, these advance-tech parents are pressuring their offspring to learn faster than their peers. Only time will tell if the emotional side effects on the children will offset the acceleration in learning. However, even those parents who have not tried to speed up their little ones into superbaby status are being swept into the race that is pushing our children toward adolescence before they have the chance to enjoy their childhood. Industry and the media have taken advantage of the trend by stepping into a very lucrative market. There are companies that sell elaborate cosmetics for four-to-nine-year-olds, and clothes manufacturers that push designer jeans and the "right labels" for everything from T-shirts to tennis shoes. Children are being programed to think their self-worth depends on what they wear or what video games they play; they look like adults and many parents treat them that way. As Dr. Elkind says, "Parents need to be adults to children and exercise parental authority, and they need to remember that kids aren't as sophisticated as they sound."[3]

Psychologists tell us it's bad to be an orphan, terrible to be an only child, damaging to be the youngest, crushing to be the middle, and taxing to be the oldest. There seems to be no way out, except to be born an adult!

The teen years do not need to be times of trouble if children are allowed to grow into them, instead of being pushed toward them prematurely.

> The teen years do not need to be times of trouble
> if children are allowed to grow into them, instead of
> being pushed into them prematurely.

PLAYING FAIR IN A
TUG OF WAR

One woman was becoming exasperated over her daughter's monopolization of the telephone, so she did what many other parents are doing these days, she had a second phone installed for her teenager's exclusive use. However, one afternoon soon after the phone was connected in her room, the mother came home to find that her phone was being used, while her daughter's stood idle. "Why aren't you using the phone we bought for you?" the mother asked through tight lips. "But, Mother, don't you see, I may get an important call, and I wouldn't want my phone to be busy!"

I have no romantic delusions that we committed Christians have the magic elixir to protect us from times of stress and strain with our teenagers. A certain amount of conflict is no indication of inadequate parenting, nor lack of faith. We need to accept the fact that in this game sometimes we're on the ground and other times we're standing up. The secret to successful parenting through those teen years is to keep our equilibrium.

The adolescent does not know whether he should act as a child or as an adult. When we disagree on his level of maturity there will be inevitable clashes. How much television should the adolescent watch? To what extent should parents supervise the movies and TV watched by a thirteen-year-old, in contrast to those watched by a sixteen-year-old? What time is the curfew? When is dating permissible? How much allowance is fair? What is the difference between the right to privacy and the need for accountability? Parents give guidance, and the child/adult says, "Don't nag me." It's been said that adolescence is the period when children are certain they will never be as stupid as their parents.

There are a few parental tips that make the rules of this tug of war we play with our teenagers a little fairer for both sides. However, we parents need to be reminded that if we haven't transgressed one or more of the principles for living with and raising teenagers, we're so perfect that we don't need to read this chapter.

Who hasn't fallen victim to the old "jump to the conclusion game"? The first tip is: *Get the facts first.* Ray and Anne Ortlund, respected Christian leaders and counselors, said that as parents of teens we have to learn not to get uptight too fast. Ray came home and found a brown bag full of beer cans in the kitchen, and his mind began to dance with fantasies and fears. When their son came home, Ray said, "Hey, what are those beer cans doing in the kitchen?" Nels said casually—and immediately Ray knew it was true—"Oh, I found them out in the yard, and I hauled them in to put in the trash compactor. Sorry I left them out—I'll go take care of it."

In retelling this episode, Ray said, "Whew! I'm so glad I didn't make a fuss first, before I got the story."[4]

Jumping to conclusions is easy to do when we have teens. Often young people say something they don't believe, because they're not sure what they do believe. They'll drop a little bombshell just to see how their parents will react. This is the time to stay cool and find out what they really mean. Solomon said,

"What a shame—yes, how stupid!—to decide before knowing the facts!" (Proverbs 18:13, TLB).

Of course, it's vital that we have facts before making judgments, but we also need to present facts when we communicate with our teenagers. "Because I say so" is an inadequate reason for a parental rule. "A rebel doesn't care about the facts. All he wants to do is yell" (Proverbs 18:2, TLB). We yell because it's easier than an explanation. We yell because we've "had it," and we say things we regret. Soon we are involved in the no-win battle of the vocal cords. We're like the mother of eight children who said, "This morning the kids were so noisy that I threatened, 'The first person in this house who screams is going to get his mouth soaped.'" Then she added, "And, you know, I can still taste the stuff!"

This may sound like a contradiction, but adolescents need to take out their frustrations on family at times because they can't do it anyplace else. If Tony yells at his friends, he may be rejected; if he yells at his teachers, he may get into trouble. But since his younger brother or sister, his mother, or even his dog, can't force him out of the group, he has a sense of power he cannot obtain anywhere else. This may be rebellion of a sort, but it doesn't indicate the family will disintegrate, or that Tony is incorrigible.

Most of us Christian parents understand that a certain amount of teenage rejection and arrogance is natural. We realize that times of crisis will come and they will pass. However, if problems seem pathological, we need to be willing to spend money for advice from Christian professionals.

How do we teach teens responsibility for their actions? I guess we've made it pretty clear that it doesn't begin at the thirteenth birthday party, rather, years earlier when we teach them the dangers of such everyday things as fire and water. That's the time we need to teach our children righteous fear. Bruce Lockerbie says:

No pleasure comes without responsibility. I tried to impress this truth on my children during their dating years. I made it very plain that in this family there would be no abortions nor financial support for any other alternative in the event of pregnancy. I told them that sexual relations meant marriage, and that they had better be prepared to face the full responsibilities for any actions they took. They knew that if they became sexually involved, they were likely to become members of their own households earlier than they had anticipated.[5]

Second tip: *Play fair with your kids by teaching responsibility in the area of sex.* How unfair we would be to toss our adolescents into a sex-saturated society without some help. How do we teach them the importance of virginity and chastity before marriage in an era which places little value on these virtues? The Bible does not provide us with specific advice on how to handle adolescents, but it does provide us with a "sound mind" ("For God hath not given us the spirit of fear, but of power, and of love, and of a sound mind" 2 Timothy 1:7, KJV) and gives us the Holy Spirit to guide us in these difficult areas. Too many parents avoid subjects because of embarrassment or personal guilt over their own indiscretions. However, early in the adolescent years is the best time to discuss sexual temptations and moral values. Take advantage of the times when communication may be more open than it will be after your adolescent enters the Great Teen Secret Society of whispered phone calls and shut doors that indicate, "I want my privacy; I'm no longer a child."

U.S. News and World Report had an article about "Telling '80s Kids about Sex" which pointed out it's not as easy today as in the "old days" before AIDS, rampant homosexuality, and sexual aberrations were reported in the media. "Surveys show that both teenagers and parents want parents, not school courses, to play the primary role in sex education. But it doesn't happen very often."

U.S. Surgeon General C. Everett Koop wrote in the article, "Parents are uncomfortable with the science of reproduction. They feel that discussion of sex is an invasion of privacy—their own as well as that of the child. And their parents didn't discuss it with them."[6]

Telling our kids about sex is vital in a society where one in every ten teenage girls becomes pregnant, and one out of seven teenagers a year contracts a sexually transmitted disease. If we wait for teenagers to bring up the subject of sex, we may wait forever. However, the world gives us many occasions for useful discussions about sex and values, if we will only take advantage of them. We can't expect classes in sex education to do the work for us.

It was refreshing to read this in a secular news magazine: "There's no compelling evidence that school classes in sex education are a force preventing teenage pregnancy and early sexual activity. The values parents instill in their children still seem to be what count most."[7]

Probably the best time for teaching a child to "just say 'No'" is long before the temptation arrives, when respect for Mom or Dad is so strong that just the thought of, "What would Dad say?" would be a deterrent to wrong behavior. One mother told me that she prayed daily for one strong role model to come into her teenagers's life, someone close enough in age to be able to relate and yet mature enough to lead. The friendship and acceptance of a Christian person their children admire can be a valuable ally for bewildered parents.

But what if one of our teens has stepped out of the boundaries of our moral standards, what then? Often they can become so trapped by guilt feelings that by the end of their adolescence they need help making the transition into a satisfactory marital relationship. Sexual instruction at this period in their lives may require the help of a Christian doctor or counselor. It is my personal plea that Christians avoid secular psychologists or psychiatrists and seek the advice of those who know biblical principles.

Third tip: *Playing fair in the parent-teen discipline game means to make the consequence fit the problem.* If teens are habitually late for dinner, have them fix their own from leftovers. It they misuse driving privileges, restrict their use of the car. When grounding is the punishment for more serious offenses, be sure that a definite, limited time is established and follow through with it. Why not ask your child, "What do you think would help you learn your lesson so you won't do this again?" If you have a good relationship, you may be surprised to find that he will come up with something stricter than what you would have imposed.

Fourth tip: *Learn the value and the limits of trust.* At the top of the pet-peeve list for most teenagers is the complaint, "My parents don't trust me." Tell your kids, "I trust you; I just don't trust your judgment." I may trust my son, but that doesn't mean I would allow him to do open-heart surgery on me. Trusting him as a person is irrelevant if his judgment or experience is not in line with what he wants to do.

> Tell your kids, "I trust you; I just don't trust your judgment."

Trust is something which is easily lost. And once it's violated by either parent or child, it's hard to regain. As parents, we need to be worthy of our kids' trust. When we are told deep, dark secrets, they should be held in confidence and not told to anyone except the Lord. I don't believe we should bring them into a prayer meeting or tell our best friend in a burst of confidentiality.

Why don't kids trust us? This lack of trust is so hard for us parents to handle, especially if we know that our teenager is taking advice from someone else. We feel threatened, or even jealous, that confidence has not been given to us.

Jay Kesler, the head of Youth for Christ and a man I respect for his counsel, says there are no easy answers to the trust question, but offers the following suggestions:

1. We shouldn't confuse their desire for independence with a lack of trust in us.
2. We shouldn't try to be infallible, instead, we can give our kids two good choices and let them choose.
3. We should be willing to tolerate conduct which differs from our own opinions (we expect them to do this) and not hold it against them.
4. We should communicate honestly and on a feeling level (e.g., "You can do this, but I'm not for it"), again letting them know it won't be held against them.
5. We should hold confidences and never share their secrets with others.[8]

"I try to be the type of person my child can trust, but I'm not sure how far to trust him. Just recently I found out that he betrayed my trust, and now I don't know if I can trust him again." This was a complaint heard from a mother, and one which is not uncommon. She has two choices: she can become hurt or angry and try to control her teen by threats, tears, or punishment, or she can use the broken trust as an opportunity to keep it from happening again. Jesus taught His disciples this principle in confronting a brother who betrayed a trust. Substitute *"child"* for *"brother"* in this verse: "If a brother sins against you, go to him privately and confront him with his fault. If he listens and confesses it, you have won back a brother" (Matthew 18:15, TLB).

Children learn to be trustworthy by being trusted. Parents who expect the best and parents who expect the worst of their teens often have their expectations come true. The parent who "thinks the worst" will usually get the worst. We do not need to be naïve, but if we know our child in his growing years, why do we expect him to change his colors when he begins to wear men's sizes? (I don't want to be accused of sexism, but I find it awkward to say "his/her" or "he/she" for every expression. Therefore I have chosen to use the universal masculine pronoun. So I ask you to put your daughter into these illustrations, as well as your son.)

BENEATH THE BRAVADO

"He's past the stage of wanting to be with us" is a common expression among parents. Teenagers have after-school activities, church activities, and part-time jobs. Their lives become as scheduled as their parents'. Scrawled notes take the place of conversation, and they eat meals on the run instead of dinner with the family. Perhaps, however, parents are too hasty in allowing their teenagers to withdraw from the family. Or maybe parents are too anxious to abdicate their own positions as parents. A grandfather told me that he was the "only male influence" in his fifteen-year-old grandson's life because the boy's father had "given up on him." Unfortunately, the grandfather lives two thousand miles from his grandson and only sees him during vacations and holidays.

A high school teacher tells about one of her students who came to school on Friday morning moaning and groaning about the fact that he had to spend Sunday afternoon at a state park with his family. He complained all day to any student or teacher who would listen. The following Monday he came in talking about the wonderful time they had hiking and climbing cliffs. It may not be "cool" to spend time with the family, but beneath the bravado is a teenager who wants his parents' time and discipline.

Deborah Bayly had been teaching high school for sixteen years when she wrote:

> Again and again I am faced with seemingly independent, sophisticated young women who dissolve into tears when they start talking about their homes. These are not abused children, nor are they what the law would call neglected. Their mothers are interested in them: They pay their tuition at the school often at considerable financial sacrifice. They come to open-house events and return teachers' phone calls. Why do the daughters of these mothers feel neglected? I believe it is because the mothers don't realize their own importance as parents. Because their children—or at least the ones who feel ignored—seem to have "grown up" just fine with

little apparent need for extra attention. The parents think their
main function is to pay the bills and put food on the table.[9]

When a teenager says, "I have to go with my folks," and makes it
sound like chewing garlic for breakfast, he probably means, "They
care enough about me to want me with them."

Recently I arranged a Sunday away from my church and our
whole family went to a large church quite a distance from our
home, and afterward we went to see "Disneyland on Ice." The
ages of our kids were: Jan, eighteen; David, seventeen; Jennifer,
twelve; and Daniel, ten. They were a little beyond the "Snow
White and the Seven Dwarfs" stage of the Disney show, but it was
fun. Also, just sitting in church with my entire family beside me,
instead of in front of me, was a real treat. I don't know if our older
kids will tell their friends about going to a program they thought
was "childish," but I know we had a ball. When we do things
together, we make a memory and that's what we'll talk about in
later years, not the struggle in trying to arrange everyone's
schedules and desires.

GIVE ME THIS DAY

What are some teen expectations for parents? These kids of ours
aren't living in an easy time, and we know it. Josh McDowell, who
has been on the campuses of 650 universities in 74 nations and
addressed more than seven million listeners, is a man whose ministry has a heart for families, and teenagers in particular. Josh
conducted a writing contest for young people and received over
one thousand letters. Parents may think that the youth of the '80s
are caught up in the self-love movement, but Josh concludes that
many of their narcissistic values are the result of self-hurt. He said
teens are overwhelmed with their own problems:

> Our children are facing difficult problems and choices much
> earlier than previous generations. . . . The top three disciplinary
> problems in school 40 years ago were listed in a survey as talking,
> chewing gum, and running in the halls. Now we're told that rape,
> robbery, and assault head the list.
> The five greatest fears of primary school children 20 years ago
> were animals, dark rooms, strangers, high places, and loud voices.

Today they're parental divorce, nuclear war, lung cancer, pollution, and muggings.[10]

The suicide rate between ages fifteen and nineteen has risen 400 percent in the last ten years. What has happened to cause this frightening epidemic? The social analysts point out the problem. An article in the *Los Angeles Times* said:

> The presence of a supportive family, whether living under one roof or two, helps teens get through adolescence. Adolescents who are without parental support may be vulnerable to impulsive, self-destructive behaviors. In addition, in families where there's little concern for adolescents by adults, early symptoms of suicidal behaviors may go unheeded. The adolescent who is neglected or unheard may see attempting suicide as the only way to get attention.[11]

Josh McDowell is convinced that parental neglect and divorce have begun what he calls a "tidal wave of emotional devastation in children who have lost their models of love." He explains,

> God intended us to learn to love Him and others by watching how our parents love each other and how they love us . . . because God is called our Father, the relationship of kids to their dads is important in their spiritual development. I believe that one of the greatest barriers to youth evangelism today is the image young people have of their fathers. Their model of fathers' love is either damaged or missing altogether.[12]

I guess if anything has become repetitious in this book, it is that parents are expected to be role models!

A teen's prayer is "Give me this day my daily dose of You and Your listening time."

One of the greatest areas of neglect with our teens is just plain fun. According to an article in *Psychology Today*, "Negative thoughts outnumber positive ones ten to one when teenagers are with their families. This may be, at least in part, because family leisure tends to consist mainly of noninteractive, unchallenging activities."[13]

Someone with a flair for the ridiculous wrote about teenage situations that provide opportunities for parents who are practical jokers. Some ideas were bizarre, even for a teenager's weird sense of humor; but others I thought were funny enough to try (although

Donna and I haven't attempted them yet). The book is facetiously called *How to Get a Teenager to Run Away from Home.* Here are some of the suggestions:

> Reset all the push buttons on his car radio so that it only gets news and classical music.
> Get a mother-daughter outfit and follow her around wherever she goes.
> Tell him you've made appointments for conferences with all his teachers.
> Make her 20 minutes early for everything by setting her clock 20 minutes ahead.
> Iron his jeans and put a crease in them.[14]

We need more laughter at a time when tears are easy to find. All of us can dream up things to do that are just plain fun.

OUT OF THE FRYING PAN

How do we prepare our teenagers for the adult world? While they're sizzling in the frying pan of the teens, soon they will be jumping into the fire of adulthood. Many of them from the protective cocoon of our evangelical shelter have not been urged, or even allowed, to take risks. I'm not talking about the risks of our suburban and urban lives that our ancestors didn't experience: drugs, muggings, sexual abuse, crime in the streets. It's the risks of men and women of achievement, those who have dared to do what others feared might lead to failure.

Joe Bayly asked, "Why have so few Christians achieved eminence in their chosen field in North America? I think one reason is that from the earliest age we've been exampled and taught to take the safe path, to avoid risks. Playing it safe is almost a tenet of our faith."[15]

If we overprotect our young people, discouraging them from trying what we have not tried, or attempting what we have not done, we may have young adults who are unprepared for the risks they face when they're on their own. Without some risk taking in life we may never experience the exhilaration of success.

Just as the ropes and pitons secure the mountain climber, we need to undergird our children in their risks by praying for their protection. We must trust our children to God for the unforeseeable risks in ordinary living, but give them the freedom and encouragement to take legitimate risks that produce great achievements.

THEY'RE WONDERFUL . . .
TELL THEM

The story is told that Michelangelo was pushing a huge piece of rock down a street. A curious neighbor poked his head out a window and said, "Why are straining over that old piece of stone?" Michelangelo is said to have answered, "Because there's an angel in that rock that wants to come out."

What treasures are hidden in those crazy, unpredictable, stimulating, baffling teens of ours? They have gifts which haven't been discovered, talents which need to be nourished, dreams to be heard.

Of course, some are well aware of their physical gifts, like the attractive teenage daughter who was accompanying her parents as they strolled around a luxurious Dallas motel. They paused beside the swimming pool just as a group of young fellows appeared, dived in, and started swimming around.

"Isn't it lovely?" the mother said.

"It certainly is," said the girl, well aware of the admiring glances she was drawing. "And Mother, they stocked it just for me!"

We need to give our kids positive reinforcement. Skip Ross says it so well in his book *Say Yes to Your Potential* when he emphasizes that the first principle for dynamic living is the principle of giving:

> What can we give out of our storehouse of talents? We all have different gifts: Some can paint, or sing, or write; others have naturally endowed skills in building, working with our hands, or understanding mathematics. However, there is one thing we all can give: Everyone can give a word of praise. You and I as humans on planet earth thrive on praise. We are built up by praise and destroyed by criticism. The writer of Proverbs says, "Kind words are like honey— enjoyable and healthful" (Proverbs 16:24, TLB).[16]

Joe Bayly once told the story about his speaking at Wheaton College's chapel service and saying that fathers of teenage girls need to tell them, "You look beautiful—I'll bet the guys in the youth group go ape over you"; and that mothers of teen-age boys

need to kiss them, "even if they have to chase them all over the
house to catch them."

What surprised Bayly was that the students applauded so long
that he couldn't continue speaking for a minute or two. After the
chapel service, a faculty wife told him, "I wish those students'
parents could have heard that applause."

Instead of telling our children what they should do and become,
we should listen to them and help them uncover the special blue-
prints God has for them.

Parents, we need to be image makers, not image breakers. Our
teens need to hear "You can do it" and "You're great."

ADDRESSED FOR SUCCESS

God has a built-in success pattern that we want for our teens,
and they want for themselves. It's included in the Father's promise
of peace, prosperity, popularity, and purpose. This formula is
packaged in the first few verses of Proverbs 3: "My son, forget not
my law; but let thine heart keep my commandments: for length of
days, and long life, and peace, shall they add to thee" (Proverbs
3:1–2, KJV).

Bumper stickers proclaim "Another Mother for Peace," and we
can't argue with those sentiments. We want our kids to have peace
in their lives, to be grateful for their heritage and content with
their circumstances. We know that until the Lord returns there
will be no peace on earth, but we do know that He gives personal
peace to His children. The Psalmist said, "The Lord will give
strength unto his people; the Lord will bless his people with
peace" (Psalm 29:11, KJV).

Not only do we want our kids to have peace, but we want them
to be healthy in order to have a long life. Teens need to be well fed;
they need to be introduced at home to nutritious food, instead of
being left to consume the junk which is abundantly supplied from
every source.

Prosperity is also a part of God's success formula—and our desire for our kids. This doesn't mean success is a guarantee, but
most kids grow up with the dream of material success. They don't
visualize themselves living in poverty, although the Lord may
sometimes put us there for a purpose. However, sometimes kids

may be confused by the patterns they see in the lives of their parents. Take for example the following scenario:

"My boy," said the father, "don't you want to succeed in life as I did?"

"Well, I don't know," the son replied, slowly. "You were raised in the country and worked and scrimped so you could go to the city. Then you slaved to own a house in the city, and almost killed yourself so you could buy this house in the country. I think I'm better off staying here than trying to make that round trip."

A person doesn't need money to be prosperous, but he does need to be generous. The principle of giving is, "Give, and it will be given to you. A good measure, pressed down, shaken together and running over, will be poured into your lap. For with the measure you use, it will be measured to you" (Luke 6:38).

Teens with a giving spirit are not trouble; they are blessings. Give them a cause to champion, a reason to sacrifice, and watch them grow tall with a feeling of accomplishment.

Popularity, as any parent of adolescents knows, ranks high in the desires of teens. And Proverbs tells us God's intentions along these lines, "So shalt thou find favor and good understanding in the sight of God and man" (Proverbs 3:4, KJV).

It's not wrong to want to be liked! In fact, this is a part of God's success formula, just as "the boy Samuel continued to grow in stature and in favor with the Lord and with men" (1 Samuel 2:26).

God also promises to give us a purpose in life, if we will follow Him. Teens with worthwhile goals avoid a lot of pitfalls. When they see a purpose for achieving their goals, they are less likely to get into trouble. Proverbs 3:6 says: "In all your ways acknowledge him, and he will make your paths straight."

Our teens are God's gift to us to feed, enjoy, test our patience, and keep our sense of humor. His desire for them is peace, prosperity, popularity, and purpose. How could we wish for anything more? As parents, we would do well to spend more time kneeling in prayer than tearing our hair.

A PARENT'S PRAYER

Make them good soldiers of Jesus Christ; let them never turn back in the day of battle. Let them be winners and helpers of souls. Let them live not to be ministered to, but to minister.

Make them loyal; let them set loyalty high above all things. Make them doers, not mere talkers. Let them enjoy hard work and choose hard things rather than easy. Make them trustworthy. Make them wise, for it is written, He hath no pleasure in fools.

Let them pass from dependence on us to dependence on Thee. Let them never come under the dominion of earthly things; keep them free. Let them grow up healthy, happy, friendly, and keen to make others happy. Give them eyes to see the beauty of the world and hearts to worship its Creator.

Let them be gentle to beast and bird; let cruelty be hateful to them. May they walk, O Lord, in the light of Thy countenance.

And for ourselves we ask that we might never weaken. "God is my strong salvation" . . . we ask that we might train them to say that word and live that life, and pour themselves out for others unhindered by self.

—AMY CARMICHAEL[17]

MYTH NINE

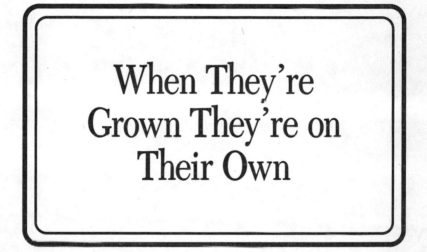

When They're Grown They're on Their Own

At the Great American Retirement Ritual, a few speeches are given about the valuable contribution the retiree has made to the company, a chicken and peas dinner is consumed, and the mystery gift is presented. The next Monday, the finality of this action is realized as Mr. Former Executive or Mrs. Ex-teacher realizes the alarm hasn't gone off and the appointment book is blank.

Parenting is one occupation where there is no such finale. After twenty or twenty-five years, no one gives us a gold engraved watch or a set of luggage for the job we've done. The kids we raised may have flown away; but, like homing pigeons, they may return to the coop to physically occupy the premises, or they may give their breeders concern because they don't return at regular intervals.

The Encyclopedia Americana describes the homing pigeons' habitat as "a loft, which is a special house or coop. The loft should be a large, airy, well-lighted room, with suitable openings for the birds to enter and leave. It should be so constructed that divisions can be provided to separate pigeons of different varieties, sexes, or ages when required." Not a bad description even for how our human pigeons come home to roost!

One of the most blatant myths about parenting is that "when they're grown they're on their own." Parenting, like war, is a lot easier to begin than it is to end. In fact, there is no armistice for parenting, just detente.

Parenting, like war, is a lot easier to begin than it is to end.

THE EMPTY NEST IS
AN ILLUSION

Parents and their offspring travel through four stages on life's journey. The first state is a time of *dependence,* when the youngster needs the parent for survival. Of all the species of life which God created, man is dependent longer than any other living creature. The next stage is the period of *independence,* when the growing child is attempting to establish his own person and pull away from the ones who have nurtured him or her. The third stage is that of *interdependence,* when the child has become an adult and is secure enough to become somewhat of a peer or friend with parents. The fourth stage—one in which we have an increasing number of adults in our society—is *reverse dependence,* when the aging parent needs the middle-aged son or daughter for emotional, and sometimes physical, survival.

However, some people get stalled along the way and never make it to stage two or three. One observer of the parenting phenomena said, "The war to attain stage two may last for fifty years, leaving both sides bitter and exhausted."[1]

Many young people today are reaching for independence while living at home. The economic squeeze has contributed to this new trend for families in the 1980s, and it's unlikely that there will be any respite from this economic dilemma in the near future. For instance, take a look at the college scene. A generation ago when Sue or Jim graduated from high school and desired to go to college it was "going away to school." Today there are junior colleges, commuter schools, and university extensions to provide the education while the kids live at home. When kids go away to school, there are many activities parents know nothing about, and it's just as well. Parents worry enough as it is. But when post-high school kids are at home, study habits, dating patterns, and social involvements may be observed at close range, just as they were in high school. And when this happens the independence stage breaks down or is delayed.

Many young marrieds are living in the old family homestead, or they are depending on Mom and Dad to subsidize the new house or apartment. When money is tight, it's difficult for parents and kids to turn loose.

BOOMERANG KIDS

We have a new category of people in today's parent-child relationships called the "boomerang kids." These are the kids who bounce back after we thought they were gone. The U.S. Census Bureau reports that 14 percent of the men and 8 percent of the women twenty-five to thirty-four years old (the "older young adults") were living with their parents in 1984, compared with 9.5 percent of the men and 6.5 percent of the women in 1970.

At a younger age, 60 percent of the men and 48 percent of the women between the ages of eighteen and twenty-four are dependent on their parents for housing (and that includes college students) compared to 54 percent and 41 percent in 1970.

"Once the adult children arrive, struggles often surface anew. Parents who were visited by the stork years before are saddled with dependents again. Feathers get ruffled easily as young and old adjust to new roles. Suddenly, returning to the nest doesn't seem like such a good idea."[2]

WHAT THE YOUNG
SINGLE FACES

When is a person "grown?" The years of maturity vary; but for the sake of defining the young single, we'll consider the years from eighteen to thirty. Dennis Guernsey, professor of marriage and family ministries at Fuller Theological Seminary, has listed seven of the tasks the young single faces as a part of the family structure.[3] This is not as formidable as it sounds.

The first task in becoming a responsible adult involves a decision to take charge of one's own life and the relationships with the people in it. This includes the relationship with God; and those who fail in this important decision may become unplugged from parents altogether or else cling to them more desperately. A vivid example of the former is the prodigal son, and the latter situation is exemplified by the elder brother in the same story.

The second task young singles face is to learn to relate to father and mother, brothers and sisters, as friends and equals. The third task (this is a tough one!) is to learn financial independence.

The fourth task singles must face is to learn functional independence—the common domestic necessities of living. Laundry isn't too tough to handle, just follow the directions; cooking is so simplified today that anyone can learn to do more than scramble eggs.

The fifth task is to seek direction for occupation or professional choices. Parents may be the best resource for advice, but additional input may come from concerned older adults who understand what the will of God is and are able to guide others in their personal search.

Singles need to prepare for marriage. And this is the sixth task. Most people do get married, even those who say they are not interested. Here's where one should never be a bargain shopper, but search out God's will for the very best quality.

As for the seventh task, Professor Guernsey says, "Look to the future." Goals are not taught in school, and one of the most difficult tasks for the "live for today" person is to be a goal-setter. Probably the best path to follow is called "flexible planning." Plan ahead, but understand that detours are a part of life's journey.

These obligations or tasks that face the young single may be seen clearly by some parents and offspring, but for others, attempts to communicate them may not be successful. Sometimes caring friends or a pastor may help, but usually the most convincing education comes from the school of experience.

BE IT EVER SO HUMBLE

If joining the real world is postponed for a time and the "kids" who are now young adults return to the sanctuary of their old rooms, what then? Rules which applied for the adolescent certainly don't apply for the young adult. One mother said, "You don't treat a five-year-old the same as you would a two-year-old, and the same holds true for twenty-year-olds and seventeen-year-olds." Curfews and reporting where they've been and with whom are not a part of the parental agenda at this stage. Rules are replaced with expectations. Parents should make clear the obligations family members have for peaceful coexistence.

One father told his daughter, who returned from college to begin work near home, "Take a few months to get some cash and buy the career clothes you need, but on the first of September, start paying reasonable room and board." A younger sister who was listening seemed shocked. "Hey, how come? You mean on August 31 she's one person, but the next day she has to pay rent?"

Her dad smiled and said, "That's right. She's got to join the real world sometime, so I'm giving four months notice."

The economic factor is only one reason for returning to the nest. What if a young person seeks the home sanctuary because his or her life is a shambles? This is a severe test that even some of the most loving parents find stressful. However, to turn away a child when he is in need is the way of the world, not the teachings of the Bible. If the young person is completely out of control, good advice is to arrange for him or her to go someplace where he can be controlled. All of us need structure in our lives, and when the walls have tumbled in on us, rebuilding them takes time.

Christian parents must learn to pass their children into the Lord's hand. One mother who had raised five children by herself was asked how she remained so calm. She said, "Well, it's because of my partner." She saw the puzzled look in her questioner's face and added, "You see, long ago I made the Lord my partner, and now I just say, 'I'll do the work, You do the worrying.' That's the only way I've been able to have peace in my life."

LEAVE AND CLEAVE

Do wedding rings and marriage vows herald the news that a young couple are on their own? When the last "I do" is said and Mom and Dad tearfully watch son or daughter shut the door on their old life, the reaction may be either a sigh of relief or a cry of anguish. "Thank God they're married; now we can relax." Or, "My little girl is gone; things will never be the same." But if you think they're "on their own," you are living a Robinson Crusoe existence. With the second and third generations, new joys are discovered and new problems are unearthed. One generation doesn't beget another generation by putting "finis" at the end of each chapter. We are part of the magnificent flow of history which makes each individual on planet earth a contributing force.

Challenges will come, and only by recognizing what they are and how they develop are we able to resolve them. The Bible gives us comfort in knowing we are not alone in our problems; others have found solutions and so can we.

Conflicts are learning experiences. If we didn't have them we would be protoplasm instead of flesh and blood. "But remember this—the wrong desires that come into your life aren't anything new and different. Many others have faced exactly the same problems before you. And no temptation is irresistible. You can trust God to keep the temptation from becoming so strong that you can't stand up against it, for he has promised this and will do what he says. He will show you how to escape temptation's power so that you can bear up patiently against it" (1 Corinthians 10:13, TLB).

Although conflicts may begin at any time, weddings are potential breeding grounds. Attitudes, jealousies, and many egos could turn the happiest day of their lives into one of the most miserable. Who is going to be invited? Who will be left out? What size or type of wedding will it be? If Father pays, do the parents have any say in how the wedding is conducted? Exhaustion and tension are multiplied by bills. And if conflicts aren't resolved at this time, the memories will linger on. Most people can describe their wedding day in detail, and one of the most important dates in a person's life should be filled with joyful memories, not bitterness.

Every wedding should be showered with a sense of humor; laughter breaks tension better than a back rub. At the end of a recent wedding ceremony, the best man and groomsmen looked at the bride, feigned the appearance of a dazzling light, and then, in unison, reached in their pockets and put on dark glasses. What a sight they were, following the newlyweds down the aisle!

During the first years of marriage, there are many potential fires with relationship adjustments. When there are parents or multiple sets of parents, where do the newlyweds spend the holidays? "Over the river and through the woods to Grandmother's house we go" is complicated by more than one set of parents.

You only need to put your particular problems in the picture to realize that being grown-up is not an independent state. Instead, it becomes more interdependent with each step in life.

AND THEN THERE WERE
THREE . . . OR MORE

Baby is born. Hallelujah, he or she is finally here. Welcome or not, the little bundle from heaven is a new burden on the backs of parents, grandparents, and assorted relatives. Intergenerational relationships are further complicated with the increase in divorces and remarriages. Let's look at some of the signs which precede conflicts in family communications and how to resolve them. It's like preventive medicine; keep healthy by knowing the sources of disease and infection and prevent them before you are sick in bed with a raging fever.

IDENTIFY CONFLICTS BEFORE
THEY BECOME PROBLEMS

Dr. Arthur Kornhaber, president and founder of the Foundation for Grandparenting, details a three-stage process describing how personal and family difficulties evolve. *The first is "open warfare."* Feuds are not limited to the Hatfields and McCoys; anyone may become involved. Brother can't stand sister, husband picks on wife, mother criticizes daughter-in-law. "In open warfare, family members are usually asked to choose sides. The family becomes polarized."[4] This is the classic beginning for a bad ending. If the limited conflict isn't resolved at this stage, a full-scale conflagration is brewing.

The next stage is more dangerous: it's when silence is not golden. When warfare has begun, the most devastating tactic is to shun the "enemy." Instead of discussing their feelings with each other, the antagonists complain to others and they avoid each other like the plague. The silent treatment is one of the deadliest weapons of all. "I never want to speak to her again." "As far as I'm concerned, he can go jump in the lake." When individuals are in this stage, communication is done by the way of a message carrier. Whoever is in the middle is usually frustrated and annoyed with both parties; however, sometimes these go-betweens can be effective in getting people back together.

Estrangement, the third stage, usually signals the end of relationships. Open fireworks have been abandoned, shunning is no longer feasible, and the tie that binds is cut in two.

If children, parents, and grandparents are alert to the signs of family warfare and put away the weapons early in the game, the deadly consequences can be avoided.

> If children, parents, and grandparents are alert to the signs of family warfare and put away the weapons early in the game, the deadly consequences can be avoided.

Psychologists may help as catalysts in relationships, friends may provide refuge and advice, and other family members may be supportive; but the real answer comes from God: "Go ahead and prepare for the conflict, but victory comes from God" (Proverbs 21:31, TLB).

If things don't get better, they get worse. Every counselor, family therapist, or mediator has used tried and true methods for people to work out their family problems. Each generation needs to learn these techniques and use them.

1. *When a problem comes up, the first thing to do is ask, "What is the problem?"* Define it, assess the situation. Solomon said to "Tackle every task that comes along, and if you fear God you can expect his blessing (Ecclesiastes 7:18, TLB). To ignore a problem is to make it worse. For some people the first instinct is to use avoidance: "If I don't think about it, it will go away."

2. *Next, what options do you have for improving the problem within the relationship?* You may go to a counselor, sit down with your pastor or a trusted friend, and try to get a perspective on yourself and your action. Write out your options and list them one by one. Some options you may believe are unthinkable, but think about them, anyhow. A mother told her daughter, who was complaining bitterly about her life, "If you are a Christian, divorce is not the answer." But the daughter put that on her options list anyhow, and began to consider what results that would bring.

3. *Next, what is the best option to choose and how could you put it into practice?* Have a plan to use the best option and communicate it directly to the person or people involved.

4. *Finally, begin working on the plan and not the problem.* If this all sounds too simplistic, it is. Most of life can be broken down into simple formulas; we just complicate things by letting ourselves get in the way. If you read through Proverbs again, you'll discover that those terse, concise verses give formulas for living which are uncomplicated.

WHAT OUR KIDS NEED
WHEN THEY'RE NO LONGER KIDS

If you have been married twenty-five years or longer, your offspring are either married, or in the upper levels of high school or college. They are in the most crucial period of their lives. Now they have the responsibility of making the decisions about their own lives, instead of relying on their parents and teachers to make those decisions for them. They are deciding about careers, companions, and courtship. Of course, that doesn't rule out in-put; a parent's experienced guidance doesn't stop when children come of age. As adult children grow older they often place great value on their parents' opinions.

My parents are in their seventies and now live in Ohio. I'm in my forties, but not old enough to keep from making them proud or breaking their hearts.

One summer I was speaking at a conference in Michigan, and one of the men on the staff, an old friend of our family, volunteered to drive me to the airport when the conference was over. As we drove, I was sharing some of the challenges we were encountering in our family, and I noticed that he had begun to dab at his eyes. Finally, he gained his composure and told me that his thirty-two-year-old daughter had called and told him her husband was leaving her and their two small children for another woman. My friend's heart was crushed.

What should we do or not do for our adult children?

1. *Our kids need our prayers, not our preaching.* Perhaps more than at any other stage of their lives, adult children need our prayers on their behalf. Sometimes we hear people say, (usually

with a resigned sigh), "I guess all we can do is pray." If we do that, it is a great deal!

When we see adult children moving in a direction we would not condone, we are tempted to immediately jump in as we have done in the past, preaching and guiding. Many parent/child relationships are broken when we try to intervene by preaching to our kids.

We also need to be careful how to report to them that we are "praying for you." The better part of discretion is pray without ceasing, but cease telling the content of our prayers.

2. *Our kids need our concern, not our control.* Remember the story I told earlier about the camping trip, when my father told our kids it was time for devotions and they said, "What's devotions?" My dad had the wisdom not to jump down my throat for neglecting what he considered essential guidance, but waited several weeks before he mentioned, "When are you and the family reading in the Bible these days?" He was showing concern, not control.

3. *Our kids need our understanding, not our undermining.* There is a term I'm hearing more and more in the vocabulary of young couples; it's expressed in reference to their own parents. The word is *manipulation.* The key weapon that is used in this tactic is guilt. As parents we can undermine our children by guilt without being conscious that we are doing it.

For instance, if there are two sets of parents to visit at Christmas, give them the freedom to choose. Mother could do an unconscious undermining by looking sad and saying, "Christmas just won't be the same without you." Or there is the telephone guilt trip: "Well, I was wondering when you would call."

Manipulation can be so subtle and so destructive that we should make every effort to examine our motives. Most of us would do well to examine 1 Corinthians 13 frequently and remember that "Love does not demand its own way. It is not irritable or touchy" (v. 5, TLB).

We need to listen before we leap. It's so neat for me to be able to sit down with my dad and just talk to him; he may not offer any suggestions, but I know he understands my struggles.

In life there will always be difficulties; however, it is through the tough times that we learn. When those times come to our adult children, we can't automatically step in as a shield, providing the money, the shelter, or the escape that we so many times would like to do. Even if it were always possible, it wouldn't necessarily be best.

Take, for example, the life of Joseph. His compassionate brother Reuben wanted to rescue him out of the pit where his jealous brothers had thrown him to die. But Joseph was sold to some traders who were passing by and taken to Egypt where he was sold once again, this time to Potiphar, Pharaoh's captain of the bodyguard. Later, Joseph was falsely accused of seducing his master's wife and sent to jail. If Joseph had been rescued from the pit or kept out of jail, he would never have learned what God wanted him to know.

Out of every adversity comes a greater reward. We cannot rescue our children from all difficulties, but we can be understanding and undergird them when circumstances are rocky.

4. *Our kids need our example, not our exhortation.* As we grow older, our kids are watching us. How does one learn how to grow old gracefully? It's by watching others. If we learn to laugh at the growing process, instead of trying to cling to youth with fingers that are beginning to lose their grip, we are making a personal statement that says, "Life is worth living, no matter how many candles are on the birthday cake." I'm not saying that growing old is not challenging, but it can be lightened with a sense of humor. Many of us recognize the signs of getting old:

- It's when everything hurts, and what doesn't hurt doesn't work.
- You get winded playing chess.
- You join a health club, and you don't go.
- You sink your teeth into a steak, and they stay there.
- The little gray-haired lady you help across the street is your wife.
- You see a pretty girl walk by, and your pacemaker makes the garage door go up.
- You bend down to pick something up, and your mind says, "Is there anything else I should do while I'm down here?"

I want to age (why grow old?) with dignity and class. We don't need to exhort our kids; we only need to live the abundant life of John 10:10, and they'll love us for it.

5. *Our kids need to see enthusiasm for life, not endurance 'til death.* It's so exciting to see an older couple who have excitement about life. How sad it is for our children to see us quit when there is so much left to live for.

John Wesley, at eighty-five, said he was not weary in traveling or preaching. He journeyed over 250,000 miles on horseback, preached over 40,000 sermons, wrote 400 books, learned and spoke 10 languages. He said he stayed young by exercise and change of air, never losing a night's sleep on land or at sea, arising at 4:00 every morning and preaching at 5:00 every morning. (When I heard the latter, I wondered who was listening at 5:00 A.M.) At eighty-seven he was annoyed that he could not preach more than twice a day and confessed to a growing urge to stay in bed after 5:30 in the morning!

At age eighty, Corrie ten Boom said she was going to write five books and do five films before she died. She did.

When, as older adults, we stop dreaming and planning, we begin to die and those around us start to die some also. We don't want to be like the anonymous man who wrote:

> Since I have retired from life's competition,
> Each day is filled with complete repetition.
> I get up every morning and dust off my wits,
> Go pick up the paper and read the obits.
> If my name isn't there, I know I'm not dead.
> I get a good breakfast and go back to bed.

6. *Our kids need our committed love, not our conditional love.*
A story that I have heard several times, and one that is supposed to be based upon a true episode, is a vivid illustration of the conditional love we must avoid.

The phone rang in a high society Boston home. On the other end of the line was a son who had just returned from Vietnam and was calling from California. His folks were more than a little conscious of their position in society—always concerned with appearances.

The boy said to his mother, "I just called to tell you that I wanted to bring a buddy home with me."

His mother said, "Of course, son, your friends are always welcome."

"Mother, there's something you need to know about this boy. One leg is gone, one arm's gone, one eye's gone, and his face is disfigured. Is it all right if I bring him home?"

His mother answered, "Well, bring him home for just a few days."

The son said, "You don't understand, Mother. I want to bring him home to live with us."

The mother began to make all kinds of excuses about what people would think, but while she was talking, the phone clicked on the other end.

A few hours later the police called from California and the mother picked up the phone again. The sergeant said, "We just found a boy with one arm, one leg, one eye, and a mangled face, who has just killed himself with a shot in the head. The identification papers on the body say he's your son."

We may never have to face such a test, but there are many other ways we may be called upon to show our committed love. What do we do when problems develop? For instance, more than ever before in the church we are faced with younger couples who go through divorce. What should a parent's responsibility to his children be when they're having marital problems?

I know a young man who was divorced and then remarried. His father would not attend the wedding because he felt his son's divorce was contrary to the Word of God. And this action built a lasting barrier between himself and his son.

We can't set an agenda for our ability to accept our children when they get older. When some parents, who raise their children in the faith, see their carefully nurtured offspring leave the faith or get involved in something else, they may withdraw their love. Too many times parents will allow disappointment like this to permanently come between them and their grown children. Our love for our grown children must be unconditional.

7. *Our kids need some protected time, not some promised time, (and so do we).* One of the things that happens when our kids grow up is that time with parents becomes more difficult. Especially as the parents grow older, I often hear, "My kids are always saying 'Let's get together,' but it's put off for another day, or another week, or another month."

When my parents lived in California, I couldn't stop my busy lifestyle to be with my mom and dad at certain times every week. However, we had almost a standing rule that every Sunday at noon we would have dinner together. We tried to make that a ritual, and I discovered that is true with other families who live in proximity. They have some particular time that is committed to spend with each other.

I began this section with "what our kids need," but parents have needs too as they grow older. Adult children and their parents need some protected times together—an appointment in the calendar, if necessary.

8. *Our kids need our cooperation, not our complaints.* When adult children reach that age called the "sandwich generation," when they are at the peak of their careers and have the pressure of raising their own young adults, parents are now older and assume a different role. Older people can become habitual complainers if they aren't careful. They see their children struggling to help them, and yet they look at life as if everything is wrong. What our kids of the "sandwich generation" need are not our complaints, but our encouragement.

It's a myth to believe that "When they're grown they're on their own," but the boomerang experience doesn't have to be bad. The positive side is that parents and adult children can come to understand each other better, to have an empathy for their individuality. Relationships may become deeper as a result. And as the former roles begin to blur, the time may come when parents are, instead, their children's best friends.

MYTH TEN

To Be Loved Is
To Feel Loved

At times, while writing about exposing the myths of parenthood, I have felt that I was exposing myself and my family by leaving the curtains open and the lights on in our home. The most vulnerable perhaps has been my daughter Jan, and for that reason, I want her to tell her story so that other young people and their confused moms and dads might have a better understanding about the most important aspect of this entire subject: love and acceptance.

You see, we parents assume that if we love our kids and show them love in the best way we know how, that they will know they are loved.

"To be loved is to feel loved" is a myth which could create a Grand Canyon in family relationships. We loved Jan just as much as our other three, but there were many times when she didn't feel loved. Feelings cannot be put into words. They are learned through experience, tested through faith, and expressed by response. Some children may experience love, but other factors crowd in to deny that experience. It's similar to our explanation of knowing the love of Jesus Christ in our lives. The facts of His love are shown in the Bible and in the expressions of His life, His death, and His resurrection. Faith is what we must have to believe in Him, and feelings are what will follow as a result.

> Feelings cannot be put into words. They are learned through experience, tested through faith, and expressed by response.

One thing we haven't explained about Jan is that we adopted her when she was a baby. She struggled because she believed she had been rejected by her real mother. From the time she was old enough to understand, we had told her that she was a very special person because we had chosen her to be our own. As a small child this fact was accepted, but when Jennifer was born and Jan was about six years old, the little doubts began to creep in. We moved to California when she was eleven, and those "feelings" of rejection, unfounded as they were, began to surface. But we promised at the beginning of this book that you would hear Jan's story, and only she can tell it as candidly as she felt it.

JAN'S STORY

"I Didn't Feel Special"

"When we moved to California I felt so alienated. I'm not like my brothers and sister, who are athletic and into all kinds of sports; I've always liked to write and draw, so when we were growing up they went outside to play while I would stay inside. I knew how important it was to my dad to be interested in sports, but I didn't want to do all those things. In fact, I didn't even like them. I felt like I wasn't somebody special, that I had really failed.

"There was always a great bond between my dad and my brothers. But sometimes it was hard for me to get his attention. I would get blank stares when he was concentrating on something, and I knew he was probably off on a sermon topic or thinking about the next football or basketball game. Sometimes I would get excited about writing a poem, but Dad couldn't get turned on by poetry like he could sports, so I'd get another one of those vague looks and he'd walk out of the room.

"I remember one time when I was *really* bugged. I was running for secretary of the school in my junior year. I didn't think there would be any question but that my parents would come to the election—they always went to all of the games of my brothers and sister. I didn't get involved with many activities, so this was a very important one for me. I won the election, but they weren't there. Maybe there was some sort of a good reason, I don't know; I was so mad I didn't even call Mom because I felt she and Dad didn't really care. I was really hurt.

"When I talked to them later, they said they didn't realize they could come. I thought, *How come you didn't ask me—you always check on the games the other kids are in.*

"It was a real struggle while I was in high school because I didn't want to go home. I didn't feel cared for by my family. My best friends were boys, 'cause I was very uncomfortable around the girls. Most of them had gone to modeling school since they were little, and their folks bought them gobs of clothes. I always had a real hard time with girls."

"Teenage Rebellion Is an Art"

"Each time I started doing something that I knew was wrong, I'd feel really guilty, then after a while I would rationalize that it wasn't so bad. But I felt lousy about myself. My self-image was a deep, deep problem, but I never told anyone how bad it was. I used to sit in my room, and for an hour or two, I would talk to myself negatively: 'You can't do anything right. Look at yourself, you're just no good.' I hated being me.

"But I grew up in a pastor's home, and I was used to putting on the front that I was really great. I went for counseling, but I didn't really listen. I was just the sweetest little girl, even though I tried to break away from this plastic face every day. Finally I discovered there was a whole person underneath that was really scared.

"When I was expelled from school, I guess I was at my lowest ebb of self-esteem. Somehow it was almost a relief that I had been caught."

"I Was So Exhausted"

"When my parents decided that the only course was for me to leave and go out of the country to school, I didn't go with my heels dug in. Looking at the situation logically, I couldn't see anything else I could do. I was under such emotional stress. I guess they were, too.

"A lot of things changed while I was in the Dominican Republic at New Horizons.[1] I'm learning a lot about relationships. Through every hardship you can always grow closer together. It's like an artist working on a sculpture; when he's chipping away, it's going to hurt because he's pounding and cutting, but the more he works, the more beautiful the sculpture will be. I think it's impossible to learn anything in life unless you encounter tough times.

"At school we had to go through some really hard physical exercises. I hated it at first—all those aerobics and push-ups . . . so many push-ups. I would hurt so much that I'd just pound on the floor and scream.

"My life was so disciplined for ten months that I was never alone. It's hard to stick to the kind of discipline we were under if you're by yourself. However, you always have rules in life and discipline is good, even though it's frustrating. Because of the structure and strictness, I will be able to keep growing. It's like exercising—even though I don't like it, I know the end result will be good.

"Because we've worked through so much, my folks say they've never felt closer to me. I feel the same way."

THE NEXT CHAPTER

Jan went from the New Horizons School to Word of Life Bible Institute. And at the latest report she is doing so well that I know God had a plan for all of us through the time of teen testing. The story is not finished, of course, but I'm grateful that she knocked this dad out of the complacent assumption that if I love my children they will know it.

How do we really convey to these wonderful kids of ours that we love them? God has the answers and the wisdom, and all I can do is claim James 1:5 every day of my life: "If any of you lacks wisdom, he should ask God, who gives generously to all without finding fault, and it will be given to him."

HOW DO WE REALLY
LOVE OUR KIDS?

What do our kids really need? More psychological counseling? More clothes or cars or stereo players? There are millions of children throughout the world who will never have any of those luxuries of life, and yet, whether they do or not, they all have the same basic craving. They want to feel loved.

How do we let them know we love them? In the only laboratory I know, my home, I've learned ten necessary ingredients which say those important three words in daily living.

1. *We love them by establishing boundaries for their lives.* When David was in sixth grade, I was helping coach the basketball team. I told him he should do his best, but I expected him to be a gentleman at all times.

One afternoon, I was picking him up at school when the principal mentioned to me that my son had been belligerent that day. As I drove home, I asked David what had happened.

"It was this way, Dad. One kid forgot all his basketball stuff and wanted to use the phone to call home. We didn't have a dime, and I tried to talk to the principal about using the school phone. He said it was against the rules, and I got real mad."

We were facing a good team the next day and needed David to play. I did a very tough thing for this basketball-competitive father and son. "David, you're not going to start," I said in the firmest voice I could command. Even though I was the coach, I was also the father who had established the boundary of behavior, and David had stepped outside of it.

A couple of years later, David was in eighth grade and playing in a tournament for Christian Junior High. On the back of their jerseys the name "Christian" was stamped to identify their school. During the tournament the referee was making some unfair decisions (we thought) and the kids started to bad-mouth the official in no uncertain terms. They went into a huddle, and I poked my head in and said, "Either you guys get your act together or change your shirts!"

Boundaries are no better than their stability under attack. It's easy to stay within boundaries if there are no temptations to step outside of them, but that's not human nature. We all know that without rules there is chaos and eventually collapse.

Dr. Joyce Brothers wrote:

> Strictness has been considered an old-fashioned method of parenting, but it may be coming back into style. A recent study of almost 2,000 fifth and sixth graders—some of whom had been reared by strict parents, others by permissive ones—produced some surprising results. The children who had been strictly disciplined

possessed high self-esteem and were high achievers, socially and academically. . . . What these children said revealed that they were actually happier than the undisciplined children. They loved the adults who made and enforced the rules they lived by."[2]

2. *We love them by enjoying them.* Kids are fun and that doesn't change when they become teenagers. Contrary to the groans from many parents, I think teenagers are great fun. When Jan was gone, I missed her laughter. It made me laugh just to hear her laugh.

David is our quiet, nonverbal son, but he has a sense of fun, too. One night we were sitting at the dinner table, discussing the latest caper by David's friends on our house; we had just undergone the tenth episode of "t.p." in only a few weeks' time. That night David and I decided to get even with his friend Courtney, who was the little schemer who had led the last raid. We lined up eight guys and spread seventy-two rolls of white toilet paper on Courtney's house. It was a masterful job. We were proud of our revenge. The only concern I had was that the pastor would get caught driving the getaway car. I could visualize the looks on the faces of some of my congregation; my image would be destroyed. But this forty-plus kid is flattered that he is accepted enough to be allowed to do those crazy, weird things with the teenagers.

I know one young couple who periodically have overripe fruit fights in their backyard with junior high kids. It's a mess, but harmless and hilarious. Which would you rather have on your lawn, toilet paper and gushy tomatoes or beer cans?

3. *We love our kids by exposing our humanness to them.* Some kids have grown up in Christian homes thinking their parents don't make mistakes. We need to let them know we're human. If you can grow up with teenagers and never have to apologize, you're not living life on the cutting edge.

One of the things Jan loves to do more than anything else is to go shopping. It is my least favorite activity in the entire world. However, there have been few common interests I have found with her during her teens, so periodically I have taken her shopping. One late afternoon there was something she "just had to have" at the mall. I had a meeting at seven o'clock, so the schedule was tight.

We agreed to meet at a certain time. (Our personal joke is that if we can't find each other in the mall, I open my wallet and she comes running.) I spent half an hour in the bookstore and then sat down on a bench to wait. When the time came for her to meet me, there was no Jan. Five, ten, twenty-five minutes passed, while I grew more irate every second. When she finally arrived, my blood was boiling. I knew I would be late for my meeting. I didn't wait for her to say a word; I just let her have it.

We climbed into the van; she was crying and I was seething. Before we pulled in the driveway, she choked a bit and said, "You didn't give me a chance to explain . . . my watch stopped."

I said, "Sure, that's a real good one." She didn't say anything more.

When we arrived home, Donna asked me what had happened, and I told her Jan had used the classic excuse that her watch had stopped. My wife gave me a strange look and said, "Honey, her watch hasn't been acting right . . . we were going to take it in for repair this week."

Believe me, I felt like a real bum. I could hear Jan sobbing in her room, so I went in, sat down on the edge of her bed, and said, "Jan, I really blew it. I want to ask you to forgive me. I was wrong and I feel terrible about it."

Similar things have happened more than once in our house. Sometimes I think mistakes are allowed so we can demonstrate our humanness to our kids. If we will not admit those mistakes and deal with them openly, we teach our children a negative lesson.

During that time of the shopping mall experience, I was preaching through the Book of 1 Corinthians. The following Sunday after my verbal explosion, the sermon topic was from 1 Corinthians 13:7 where it says that love believes all things. *The Living Bible* says: "If you love someone you will be loyal to him no matter what the cost. You will always believe in him, always expect the best of him, and always stand your ground in defending him." Just then I spied Jan in the audience, saw her poke one of her friends and whisper something in her ear. Would I have been in trouble if I had not taken care of my apology the week before!

4. *We love our children by explaining our reasons for decisions.* Many of you may have grown up in a home where you were told, "We don't have to explain it to you; we're telling you. You do it because we said so." It's true, as parents we do have that right, but if we do that often we leave a root of bitterness that grows and may become a rebellious heart.

When I was growing up, we didn't go to movies. However, when we moved to California, I soon discovered they are not an issue in most churches; they were just accepted as the norm.

Jan was in junior high when she came to me and said, "I want to go to the movies." I really couldn't answer her immediately, so I said, "Let me think about it."

I knew I was outdated with such an archaic attitude, and I certainly couldn't cite chapter and verse where there was anything wrong, but I was truly bothered about this decision. Finally I said to Jan, "I'm not sure I won't reevaluate this, but, Honey, let me tell you where I stand. When I was growing up that was a door that was never opened in my life. I've had a lot of problems and temptations, but none of them have to do with going to movies and filling my mind with the stories and images on the screen. What you're asking me to do is open that door for you, and I'm just not willing to do that right now. Does that make sense?"

She shrugged her shoulders and said, "Okay, Dad," and went on to another subject. We rent movies and have movie parties in our house where the subject matter and atmosphere are in our control. I'm not saying that is for everybody, nor would I want to suggest that this is the only logical response to what is presented in screen entertainment, neither am I implying that Jan's response is one you will always get.

Some time after Jan's original movie request, one of her teachers told me that she had taken a lot of abuse from her peers because she wasn't allowed to go to a show. At that time the teasing didn't sway her.

5. *We love our kids by exchanging ideas with them.* Teenagers have a bizarre way of trying to communicate. Sometimes we think they're speaking another language—one we need to go to linguistics school to understand. However, it's crucial that we listen and exchange ideas with them when they're available.

Other times we parents tend to concentrate on secondary issues and by-pass the vital. We concern ourselves with hair styles and rock music, when the real problems are with sex, drugs, alcohol, depression, and personal relationships. One educator said to me, "Matters which are really crucial for pastors and youth leaders to speak to these kids about are lost in all of the other negative agenda, so the kids are soon tuning out everything we say."

I believe we need to reserve judgment for things which are

absolutely crucial and exchange ideas with our children on those subjects where generations differ.

6. *We love our kids by encouraging them.* A group of seventh-through-ninth-grade kids were expelled from school for drinking. One of them was a sweet little girl I knew, so I asked David how on earth she had become involved in this scene. He said, "She just wanted to be one of the gang." Kids are so concerned about being accepted by their peers that they fail to recognize their own potential. When we see our emerging adults struggling with self-esteem, we need to be their greatest fans. They need every boost we can give them. Encouragement is the nutrition our spirits thrive on.

Rich DeVos, the co-founder of one of America's great companies, was asked what management skill was the most valuable for a leader to have, and he said, "Be a cheerleader." That also applies to the management of a family. Far too many of us join the booing section or become referees instead of being the head cheerleader.

7. *We love them by expanding their horizons.* Our children's dreams are so important. Encouragement is vital during times of defeat, but we need to help them look beyond today to their promise of future accomplishments. Expanding horizons isn't just exposing them to travel or music or art, but giving them visions of where they might go or be if they head in the right direction.

8. *We love them by expressing physically what we feel in our hearts.* I've found that the hardest time to hug a daughter is when she is a teenager. When she is a cute baby or a little girl, it's easy, but when she begins to emerge as a young woman there is a certain reticence which builds. However, it is then that she needs her dad the most.

We've talked about the importance of the relationship between a dad and his daughter, and I continue to believe that at the teen years a girl needs her dad even more than her mother. (But, Mothers, please don't use that as a chance to abdicate.)

Donna said, "I had her until she was thirteen; she's yours now." From then on, Jan had to come to me for major decisions. When I told her no, she would accept it, but when Donna did, World War III broke out.

We need to be huggers. With the boys we can punch each other and it's a show of affection, but our girls need their hair stroked or a bear hug. The bumper stickers, "Have you hugged your child lately?" are good reminders of an important action.

A friend of ours said she used to hug her boys when they stood like telephone poles. Now they are past the adolescent stage and they hug her back. Patience pays.

A headline in a San Antonio paper announced that "Four Hugs a Day Chase Blues Away!" The writer said, "I suspect society at large suffers from low-grade, chronic hug deficiency, and we don't even know it."

9. *We love our kids by examining our own lives regularly.* One of the best things I can do for our kids is to love my wife and keep my life clean before the Lord. The picture of life our children see is the one we present to them. We have such a short time to influence and help mold them into men and women of God.

10. *We love our kids by exercising great patience with them.* The Bible says, "The Lord is not slow in keeping his promise, as some understand slowness. He is patient with you . . . " (2 Peter 3:9).

As a sign in a Texas country store said, "Be patient. None of us am perfect."

HE'S NOT THROUGH
WITH ME YET

We began this book with the story of what appeared at the time to be a tragedy. It was the day my initial dreams for one of my children exploded in front of me. Many months have passed since then, and I have come to appreciate how God uses different experiences to cause us to grow and to enable us to love our children in a way we couldn't without such experiences.

Malcolm Muggeridge said it so well when he gave the following testimony:

> Contrary to what might be expected, I look back on experiences that at the time seemed especially desolating and painful with particular satisfaction. Indeed, I can say with complete truthfulness that everything I have learned in my seventy-five years in this world, everything that has truly enhanced and enlightened my existence, has been through affliction and not through happiness, whether pursued or attained. In other words, if it ever were to be possible to eliminate affliction from our earthly existence by means of some drug or other medical mumbo jumbo, the result would not be to make life delectable, but to make it too banal and trivial to be endurable.[3]

My relationship with Jan is what it is today because of the trouble we have seen together. The moments I remember with my oldest son, David, when he was experiencing difficult times with his brief athletic career, are times that have bonded us.

With Jennifer, there was a time when I got a phone call saying she had been seriously hurt while playing soccer on the playground. We took her to the hospital with a concussion and partial memory loss; a neurologist was consulted and said she should stay in the hospital for several days. Jennifer was a very frightened little girl, and Donna and I took turns staying with her all night. My role as a father was just to continually reassure her it was going to be okay, and, of course, it was. We grew very close during that experience.

With Daniel, our accident-prone kid, there have been so many emergencies that the Parkview Emergency Hospital in Fort Wayne knew us by our first names. One night Daniel was flying through the living room, fantasizing the NFL, and made a 20-foot flying leap into the end zone, only the end zone happened to be a stone wall. I do not want to suggest to Daniel that he continue these hospital trips. We love him enough without the trauma.

In the early days of my ministry I remember getting on airplanes to go for speaking engagements in other cities, lacking in faith that God could care for my children in my absence. As I have grown in the Lord, I have seen His faithfulness in so many ways and have been able to trust my children to His care.

If I had to pick one particular experience when my family seemed most important to me, I suppose it would be the day that left me emotionally about the same way as the moment we described in the first chapter.

We had started our ministry in California and had worked through some of the initial transitional challenges. After some changes in personnel that were not popular with some of the people in the church, we were under fire and feeling the heat intensely.

One afternoon, as I came out of my office, I discovered my faithful secretary, Glenda, very upset about something that had just happened. When I quizzed her, she reluctantly told me about a phone call from one of the rather angry people who was in the congregation at that time. He reported that he had a petition with about a hundred names on it and was coming to the business meeting to demand my resignation.

Donna was in the outer office that day, and when I finished hearing this news I brought her into my office and closed the door.

As I fought back my emotions, I said, "Donna, I have no idea what is going to happen tonight. We just received a phone call that Mr. _____ has a petition calling for my resignation. I'm sorry I brought you into this situation and have jeopardized our security. Only God knows what is going to happen tonight."

She never hesitated. "That's one thing you don't have to worry about. The kids and I are not concerned about our future; it's a future with you. God will always have a place for you, and we love and believe in you more than you will ever know."

We prayed and cried together . . . it left a deep and precious memory of a wife and family who loved me and would stand with me. Everything I had hoped for in my life in the ministry seemed endangered by a piece of paper, but it didn't really matter. I had Donna and four children whom I deeply loved and who loved me. Whatever else was going on in the world outside of that intimate circle seemed relatively unimportant. When I was hurting, I had a partner who was not only able to say, "I love you," but to make me feel it at a level I could use.

For a brief time after our business meeting started that evening, I glanced at the door, expecting a man to walk in with a list of people who did not want me as their pastor. However, I had ceased to feel threatened, for my wife's love had given me the assurance I needed. The minutes and hours ticked away and no one came; the petition never materialized. Donna's acceptance of our future together, no matter what might happen, was the unswerving faith I needed at that moment in my life.

It's a myth to believe that just because we are loved, we feel loved. To love others is not enough! Somehow we must make them feel that love, because the only kind of love we can use, is the love we can feel.

> To love others is not enough! Somehow we must make them feel that love, because the only kind of love we can use, is the love we can feel.

PARABLE OF THE SAD LITTLE GIRL

I will never forget how powerfully this truth about love came home to me several years ago when I read a parable entitled. "A Certain Man, a Little Girl, and a Horse." The parable was written by a minister and delivered for the first time in the chapel service of the Yale Divinity School. More than anything I have ever heard, it expresses the importance of drawing near to our families—so near that our love can actually be felt.

There was a certain middle-class suburban pastor who lived with his little girl in a seven-room parsonage. When the child was only four years old, her mother died. After that the little girl was unusually sad. She seldom smiled or laughed, never put her arms around anyone, played alone in her room for hours on end, and talked quietly to herself as she fell asleep each night. No matter how bright the sun shone in the morning, at breakfast in that parsonage a gloomy little voice would report, "I feel sad; I always feel sad. You know that, Daddy, so why do you always ask? I wish I could be born all over again."

Accompanying the sadness of this little girl was her insatiable desire to own a horse—not a hobbyhorse, nor a stuffed horse, nor one you pull across the floor on a string, but a real live horse. She couldn't seem to accept the fact that there was no way to house a horse in the parsonage. She only felt that it would fill some of the emptiness she was too young to describe.

When the little girl's mother had become seriously ill, everyone was very brave about it; they put on their very Christian, very cheerful faces and never cried around the little girl. Everyone talked about how happy a place heaven was and told her that her Mommy wouldn't hurt anymore. Her father thought that was the sensible way to handle the whole affair.

Mommy had been very courageous, and part of her courage through her long and painful illness had been to help the little girl become accustomed to getting along without her. As soon as she knew she was going to die, she began inviting different friends and nursemaids to take the little girl on holidays and for long weekends.

Her mother had really wanted to gather her daughter in her arms and laugh and cry with her, to tell her how much she loved her, but she had known she would soon be leaving this world and thought

the least she could do was not allow the child's attachment to grow
too strong. And so she had finally died, leaving husband and child to
comfort each other the best they could.

The little girl's father tried to be affectionate, but she was not
normally a very loving child, and he thought he was being sensible
not to force himself on her. After all, she squirmed and complained
that his whiskers scratched when he kissed her, so he gave that up,
too.

All of this happened before one particular night when this pastor was very wearily putting his little girl to bed. Although she was
in one of her uncooperative moods, he finally got her tucked in
and knelt to hear her prayers. As usual, they were very proper
prayers: "Now I lay me down to sleep. . . ." But on this night, the
tragic dimension of the child took over. She launched out on her
own, apart from the memorized prayer, and began to plead, "Dear
God, help me not to always feel so sad."

Her father felt a tear in his eye and another roll down his cheek.
He was alarmed, for he thought, "If she knows I am crying, her
world will surely tumble in. I must be composed and sure for her
security." But it was too late. A tear once shed cannot be recalled,
and one had gone quite out of control and fallen on the child's face,
deep in her cuddly blanket.

"Daddy, you're crying," she said.

"Oh, no, my dear," came the false assurance. "Go to sleep now,
pleasant dreams."

"But you are crying," she said, not with alarm, but with curiosity.

He could not keep the pose any longer. After all, he had some
respect for the truth. "Well, just a tear or two tonight," he said.
And then, with almost angry self-assertion, he added, "It's just
possible, you know, that Daddy feels sad sometimes, too."

"You do?" She paused for a moment and wrinkled her little
brow. "What about? Mommy?"

"Yes, about Mommy sometimes. I miss her very much."

"Is that what you're crying about tonight?" she asked.

"No, dear," he said, almost before he realized what he was doing,
"tonight I feel sad about you . . . about your feeling so sad. I love
you so very much that it hurts, hurts awfully that you are so sad
and. . . ."

Then he paused. He had said too much. How could he repair
the damage to her security? The silence between them was

awkward, and it seemed very long. Finally, he stood and bent over the bed and tucked her in briskly, reassuringly. But before he could straighten up and leave the room, she reached her arms around his neck and kissed him on the most prickly part of his day-old beard. Almost at once she pulled her blanket under her chin and closed her eyes. She didn't talk to herself, as she had so many nights before, and a little smile curved the corners of her mouth as she settled down to sleep.

It's really rather strange, but ever since that night, the little girl never again talked about wanting a horse.[4]

A SPECIAL KIND OF LOVE

As I think of the many thoughts we have tried to communicate in this book, I realize the most important thing I could ever say is this: If you have a family and you love them, you are rich, but don't forget to enrich them as well by making sure that the love you have in your heart is felt by each and every member of that family at the deepest level of their lives.

Communicate that love to them now; don't wait for the difficult times. Make sure the love bond is strong and the cords are woven tight.

"All the special gifts and powers from God will someday come to an end, but love goes on forever" (1 Corinthians 13:8, TLB).

Notes

Myth One. *Good Parents Don't Have Problems with Their Kids*

1. John White, *Parents in Pain* (Downers Grove, IL: Inter-Varsity Press, 1979), 43.
2. Evelyn Christenson, "Advice for Discouraged Parents," *Parents and Teenagers* by Jay Kesler (Wheaton, IL: Victor Books, 1985), 74.
3. James Dobson, *Dr. Dobson Answers Your Questions* (Wheaton, IL: Tyndale House, 1982), 465–466.
4. Joe Bayly, "Don't Stop Loving Your Children," *Family Life Today*, July/August, 1986, 9.
5. Anthony Campolo, *Deadly Sins* (Wheaton, IL: Victor Books, 1987), 21.

Myth Two. *Time: It's Not the Quantity, But the Quality*

1. B. G. Brown, *Vital Speeches*, 1961, 702.
2. James C. Dobson, *Straight Talk to Men and Their Wives* (Waco, TX: Word Books, 1980), 35–36.
3. "Child's Cry" by Dennis Agajanian, copyright © 1981 by Communiqué Music, Inc./ASCAP. All rights reserved. Used by permission of Spectra Copyright Management, Inc., Nashville, TN.
4. Catherine Marshall, *A Man Called Peter* (NY: McGraw-Hill, 1951), 57.
5. Prudence Mackintosh, "The Myth of Quality Time," *Ladies' Home Journal*, May 1984.
6. From "We Have This Moment Today" by William J. and

    7. Used with permission of Paul and Teri Reisser.

Myth Three. *She's Mommy's Girl*

    1. William S. Appleton, M.D., *Fathers and Daughters* (Garden City, NY: Doubleday & Company, 1981), 31.
    2. Bill Cosby, *Fatherhood* (Garden City, NY: Doubleday & Company, 1986), 129.
    3. Stella Chase, M.D. and Jane Whitbread, *Daughters from Infancy to Independence* (Garden City, NY: Doubleday & Company, 1979), 222.
    4. Alexandra Symons, "How Fathers Influence Daughters," *Los Angeles Times*, 6 April 1983, Part IV.
    5. V. B. Carter, *Winston Churchill As I Knew Him* (London: Evre, Stotheswoode, and Collins, 1965), 27, 28.
    6. M. J. Sobran, *Fatherhood* (New York: The Human Life Foundation, Inc.) vol. IV, no. 2, 44.
    7. Phyllis Theroux, "The Father-Daughter Dance," *McCall's*, June 1978, 78.
    8. Symons, "How Fathers Influence Daughters."
    9. David B. Lynn, *Daughters and Parents*, (Monterey, CA: Brooks/Cole Publishing Company, 1979), 125.
    10. Suzanne Fields, *Like Father, Like Daughter* (Boston: Little, Brown & Co., 1983), 69.
    11. Appleton, *Fathers and Daughters*, 12.
    12. Lynn, *Daughters and Parents*, 125.
    13. Maureen Green, *Fathering* (New York: McGraw-Hill, 1976), 102.
    14. Ibid., 96.
    15. *Newsweek*, 16 Jan. 1984, 78.
    16. *Los Angeles Times*, 6 April 1983, Part V.
    17. *Newsweek*, 16 Jan. 1984, 78.
    18. Green, *Fathering*, 97.
    19. *Time*, 12 Oct. 1987, 71.

20. *Ladies' Home Journal,* May 1980, 171.

21. Thomas Howard, "The Yoke of Fatherhood," *Christianity Today,* 23 June 1978.

22. Charlie Shedd, *Smart Dads I Know,* (Mission, KS: Sheed Andrews & McMeel, Inc., 1975), 85, 87.

23. "Her Daddy's Love," by Steve and Annie Chapman. © Copyright 1983 by Dawn Treader Music. All rights reserved. Used by permission.

Myth Four. *He's Daddy's Boy*

1. Billy Graham, *Facing Death* (Waco, TX: Word Books, 1987), 179–180.

2. Edith Deen, *All of the Women of the Bible* (New York: Harper & Brothers, 1955), 157.

3. Herbert Lockyer, *All the Women of the Bible* (Grand Rapids, MI: Zondervan, 1978), 98.

4. *Time,* 22 June 1987, 54.

5. Ibid., 56.

6. Peyton Bailey Budinger, "The Girl Inside the Woman," *Reader's Digest,* April 1984, 60.

7. Louise Neph, *Home Life,* September 1974.

8. Paul Meier and Richard Meier, *Family Foundations—How to Have a Happy Home* (Grand Rapids, MI: Baker Book House, 1981), 67–68.

9. "O, Zion Haste," a hymn by Mary Ann Thompson, 1870.

Myth Five. *A Chapter a Day Keeps the Devil Away*

1. Edward Thornton, *Raising God Consciousness in the Family* (source unknown).

2. Paul Meier and Richard Meier, *Family Foundations—How to Have a Happy Home* (Grand Rapids, MI: Baker Book House, 1981) 97–98.

3. H. Dennis Fisher, "Jewish Lessons for Disciplining Children," *Discipleship Journal*, no. 30 (1985): 40.

4. Dale Evans Rogers, *Grandparents Can* (Old Tappan, NJ: Fleming Revell, 1983), 12.

Myth Six. *Read a Book and Raise a Child*

1. Leah Yarrow, "Which Kind of Parent Are You, Strict or Permissive?" *Parents* July 1979, 49.

2. Gene Getz, *The Measure of a Family* (Glendale, CA: Regal Books, 1976), 112.

3. David Jeremiah, *The Wisdom of God* (Milford, MI: Mott Media), 63.

4. James Dobson, *Dare to Discipline* (Wheaton, IL: Tyndale Publishers, 1971), 29, 30.

5. Getz, *The Measure of a Family*, 119.

6. Gary Smalley, "Overcome the Major Destroyer of Families" *Evangelizing Today's Child*, Nov./Dec. 1985, 13.

7. Ibid., 13–15.

Myth Seven. *TV Doesn't Affect Me*

1. *U.S. News & World Report*, 2 August 1982, 28.

2. Ingrid Groller, "TV and Family Life: Do They Mix?" *Parents*, May 1987, 32.

3. Ibid.

4. Ibid.

5. Harry F. Waters and Mark D. Vehling, "Toying with Kids' TV," *Newsweek*, 13 May 1985, 85.

6. Neala Schwartzberg, "What TV Does to Kids," *Parents*, June 1987, 102.

7. Ibid., 103.

8. Clement G. Walchshauser, "The Mass Hypnotic," *Fundamentalist Journal*, Oct. 1984, 46.

9. "Johnny Can't Write Either," *Consumer's Research*, August 1987, 36.

10. Ibid., 21.

11. John D. Graham, "Spoiled Grapes," *Fundamentalist Journal*, Oct. 1984, 30.

12. Maureen Hay Read, "Is There Life without Television?" *Decision*, Jan. 1988, 29.

13. Judy Gaylin, "TV Cold Turkey," *Parents*, Sept. 1987, 103.

14. Ibid., 104.

15. Henry Baron, "TV Bondage: Breaking the Chains," *Christian Home & School*, March 1984, 14.

Myth Eight.   *Teens Are Trouble*

1. Ronald Koteskey, "Growing Up Too Late, Too Soon," *Christianity Today*, 13 March 1981, 24.

2. David Elkind, "Don't Rush Your Child," *People Weekly*, 23 April 1984.

3. Ibid.

4. Jay Kesler, ed., *Parents and Teenagers*, (Wheaton, IL: Victor Books, 1984), 419.

5. Bruce Lockerbie, "Teaching Teens Responsibility for Their Actions," in *Parents and Teenagers*, ed. Jay Kesler, 420.

6. *U.S. News and World Report*, 16 Nov. 1987, 83.

7. Ibid., 84.

8. Kesler, ed., *Parents and Teenagers*, 434.

9. Deborah Bayly, "The Bayly Wick," *Family Life Today*, March 1986, 9.

10. Paul Thigpen, "Josh McDowell, a Heart for Families," *Christian Life*, Oct. 1986.

11. *Los Angeles Times*, 17 March 1987, Part V, 8.

12. Thigpen, "Josh McDowell, a Heart for Families."

13. Alfie Kohn, "Teenagers Under Glass" *Psychology Today*, 18, no. 7, (July 1984):6.

14. Martin Ragaway, *How to Get a Teenager to Run Away from Home*, (Los Angeles: Price/Stern/Sloan, 1983).

15. Joe Bayly, "Risks Are for Kids," *Eternity*, May 1985, 64.

16. Skip Ross, *Say Yes to Your Potential*, (Waco, TX: Word Books, 1983), 55.

17. Amy Carmichael, "A Parent's Prayer," *Partnership*, May/ June 1986, 31.

Myth Nine. *When They're Grown They're on Their Own*

1. Dean Merrill, *Today's Christian Woman*, Nov./Dec. 1983, 74.
2. "For Some Families, Leaving the Nest Has Ups and Downs," *San Diego Union*, 10 Jan. 1988.
3. Dennis Guernsey as quoted by Dean Merrill in "Well Done, Thou Good and Faithful Parent," *Today's Christian Woman*, Nov./ Dec. 1983, 74.
4. Arthur Kornhaber, M.D., *Between Parents and Grandparents* (New York: Berkeley Books, 1986), 96.

Myth Ten. *To Be Loved Is To Feel Loved*

1. New Horizons Youth Ministries, 1000 South 350 East, Marion, Indiana 46953.
2. Dr. Joyce Brothers, "The Power of Love," *Good Housekeeping*, Sept. 1985, 103.
3. Malcolm Muggeridge, *A Twentieth Century Testimony* (Nashville, TN: Thomas Nelson Co., 1978), 18.
4. Adapted from: Barr Brown, "A Certain Man, a Little Girl, and a Horse," *Christian Century*, 3–10 June 1981, 643. Used by permission.